L

S

From the same author - 2010 - *Rip Off Your Necktie and Dance,* Global Professional Publishing, ISBN: 978-1906403690.

First published by Global Professional Publishing Limited 2012

Global Professional Publishing and the author believe that the sources of information upon which the book is based are reliable, and have made every effort to ensure the complete accuracy of the text and proper use of screen captures from companies' public websites in order to provide clarification and inspiration to the reader. However, Global Professional Publishing, the author and any contributor cannot accept legal responsibility for consequences that may arise from errors or omissions or any opinion or advice given.

Enquiries to the publisher at
the address below:

Global Professional Publishing Limited
Random Acres
Slip Mill Lane
Hawkhurst
Cranbrook
Kent TN18 5AD
UK

Email: publishing@gppbooks.com

Dutch editing: Alice Schulingkamp
English editing: Jack Gocher
Chapter 3, 8 and 12: Jason Fazackerley
Chapter 4 and 5: Geerd Schlangen
Chapter 9: Jeroen Verkuyl
Chapter 10: Herman van Leeuwen
Design:
Barnyard (Frans Mooren, Marcel Boshuizen)
Printed on FSC accredited ECF paper.

ISBN 978-1-906403-89-8

LEEN ZEVENBERGEN

Sustainability @ the Speed of Passion!

ORGANIZE **WOW & FLOW** IN YOUR BUSINESS

GLOBAL
professional
publishing

Content

你的努力不應只為了自己的利益

SUSTAINABILITY @ THE SPEED OF PASSION!

'The future may be made up of many factors but where it truly lies is in the hearts and minds of men. Your dedication should not be confined for your own gain, but unleash your passion for our beloved country as well as for the integrity and humanity of mankind.'
(Li Ka Shing, Chinese Businessman)

Before I started with this new book it was important to share my enthusiasm with many people. When energy is building up to write, to be inspired and to inspire other people and to put lots and lots of energy in a big piece of work, one talks. One talks, one listens and one dreams, and these dreams are big. These dreams are the dreams of success in a sense that people read the book, get inspired and use its ideas. So, one talks.

'Yes, I am working on a new book and it should be great (of course it is going to be great. How can you start working on something, thinking that it is not going to be good and great, that it's a piece of shit), and its about sustainability. To be more specific, its about how you should build sustainable companies because there are not enough of them and its hard and...'

This is where people interrupt me by saying: 'But there are more than enough books about that already, and besides that Leen, sustainability is over. It's a non-issue nowadays, because everybody already is sustainable. And companies have other things to do than sustaining their businesses – *crisis*. Don't waste your time Leen and do something more useful than sustainability. The word alone, ouch, is so 2011.'

That really is motivating me!! Sustainability is over. Every company already is sustainable. And has other things to do. Many books are written about this topic already. These are like comments that you should not start your own company when there is a crisis. Of course you should start in the bitter depth of a crisis, that is the ultimate moment. Build success right from the bottom.

Didn't I tell you all that I get my biggest motivation from people who tell me that my dream is impossible, that my dream is over and old-fashioned. When in 1984 I started my first company, people told me that the area in which I started my company, being Artificial Intelligence (AI), was over and many years behind us. Later on, in 2011, the heydays of AI started. You see, one can be early with a dream, but never too late.

Sustainability is over.

'I am getting sick of that word, it doesn't mean anything and everybody is using it nowadays.' Who said that again? I am getting sick of it, right. Sick of the fact that nobody is doing a thing but everybody is talking about it. Is that what you mean, huh?

Now, let me tell you one thing; Hardly any company is doing real work on sustainability and we have seen nothing yet in terms of real results. Is that clear to you? Is that bloody clear enough?

Are you making me mad? Yes, I believe so. I believe that I am getting a little upset here, by the fact that people seem to be thinking that sustainability is something that will go away, that it is a word which doesn't mean anything anymore because it has been misused and abused over and over again.

I have worked in normal companies my whole life, always as the CEO or leader. Whatever. I do not know anything else than running companies and I know very many companies on the highest level. I see how companies are being run and I see ambitions of managers and sometimes entrepreneurs. Different types, I tell you, believe you me.

I'll tell you, whatever we say we won't get rid of sustainability. And if you're on the other side – you believe that People are part of sustainability as one of the three P's, then there is a hell of a lot of work to be done to become sustainable. We are not even talking about the Planet P yet, because the People P in itself is causing so many problems that I hardly have any hope for companies to ever become sustainable.

Mentioning the People P and the Planet P here brings to mind that there is another P, the Profit P, which is the big hideaway for people who just do not want to care. 'Yeah Leen, just make a profit boy, and then we will talk about other things.' Yeah, right, just make a profit first, sounds reasonable doesn't it? It does, it really does, we should make a profit first, definitely in an era in which companies need to survive, we call it a crisis.

So, in the company I am running now, our first and foremost goal is to become profitable. And slowly but surely we are doing that very thing. But, becoming profitable can be done in many ways. And it seems smart to me to become profitable in such a way that we lay the grounds for sustainability as well.

And I tell you, since my current company is a public company, it is extremely difficult to make it sustainable. Crisis, green washing, public company... Maybe this is no coincidence? Maybe it had to be that I am running the most difficult company to make sustainable. Maybe it is near to suicide. Maybe that is how it was meant to be.

You see, I am a big believer in synchronicity. Synchronicity means that 'coincidence does not exist'. Way too often it happened to me in my life that I thought 'how is this coincidence possible?' Well, it isn't, because it is.

> Synchronicity means that 'coincidence does not exist'.

And I am running a public company now, which has to report every three months. So what about sustainability? Sustainability means that you should have some form of long-term orientation. Like the Mars family has. The largest family owned business is thinking in 30-year terms and we are thinking in 3 months. What about long-term?

But the challenge is there. Just there. Would it be possible, even for a public company, to be sustainable? Is that not the most difficult environment to be sustainable? Would this not be THE place where I need all my experience that I have collected over the past 25 years? Is that not why I am here?

The answer doesn't matter very much, yes or no, it doesn't matter, because I am here anyway and I only want to work for and be in a company that is 100% sustainable. So... build it.

This book that I am writing is willing to help anybody who really wants to make her or his company sustainable. So it has to be pragmatic and true. It has to give a true picture of what the difficulties are that you run into when you really want to do the job. It has to show why it might seem impossible; it should give energy when you think you are destined to fail; it has to explain go-arounds when you are blocked by management; it has to give inspiration that you can use to inspire your friends and enemies; it brings you to unknown websites and books; you should be able to give it to others to bring them into the game and it should be passionate.

Well, quite a goal for a new book, which is totally different from books I have written before. My book 'Rip Off Your Necktie and Dance', showed how the People P should and can be handled and was quite a success in many countries. Surprisingly so, because one would think that everything I wrote in that book is well known to all of you. It was indeed, but everything in that book was known to all managers, but hardly ever practiced. It's only now that companies start looking at it. Very carefully of course. Yeah, one can be early. Told you so.

Reality is tough, because it is extremely hard, if not impossible, to turn existing companies into sustainable companies. One needs to be radical, as Ray Anderson showed at Interface. Radical is the right word. Radical is a very nice word if you think about it. It shows power, force, endurance and passion. Radical people are definitely passionate. And that is where Passion comes in.

Very early in the process of writing this book it struck me. It really struck me hard, that Passion is the most crucial element in becoming sustainable.

Theoretically sustainability has to do with the three P's, people told me. 'Yes Leen, when you want to build a sustainable company you have to work around the three P's of Profit, People and Planet.' I have been to many conferences, platforms, user groups etc., all talking about these three P's. All great meetings, I have to admit, all visited by people who were convinced. All singing the same song of sustainability. Mostly agreeing, but not always.

10

But it struck me in the beginning process of writing this book that the most essential element was missing. Nobody was talking about the most elementary part of becoming sustainable. Hardly anyone is busy with the most elementary. And that most elementary part is Passion.

Building sustainable companies, building sustainable organizations, building anything sustainable requires Passion. Believe me, when Passion is not there, when it is not real and does not come from the heart, there will be no sustainable sustainability. The process that you start will fade away after a while. Passion gives you the energy you need to keep on going. Ray Anderson could never have kept up his dream if he had not been passionate and neither can I.

So, when talking about sustainability we need the four P's; Passion, People, Planet and Profit. Because that in my opinion is the right order of things. Well, where did the Passion go?

The Passion P is so obvious, so essential, that it was simply forgotten. It is gone. Actually, it was never there.

And with this book I want to bring the Passion back into the equation. Therefore every chapter should hit you hard by way of the Passion in it. Passion can only be in a book when it is in the writer. Or in the writers. Yeah, I am not writing this book alone, as I am not sustaining our company and our business alone. Progress in sustainability can only be made together with others, other passionate persons. Together we've brought up the topics, all based upon personal experiences and real life examples. Issues that were already in our heads and hearts and just had to be put on paper. It was there already, but not on paper yet. So this book is directly from the heart, believe it or not. Do with it what you want, or just do not use it. Fine with me, whatever you decide.

I just know that hundreds of thousands of people are working for companies that have a wish to become sustainable. Most of these companies run their daily business, which blocks the process of moving forward on sustainability. All of them realize that you have to fight and fight again, in order to stay on the track. And in doing that you need one thing; energy. Energy that you get from your own Passion or the Passion of others.

Bring that Passion back into the process, find the lost P of Passion.

From now on we all will define Sustainability as the four P's; Passion, People, Planet, Profit. With our Passion we inspire People to care for the Planet and to become Profitable with it. Simple, huh?

This book is produced in a different way than my earlier books. Some friends were so very inspired by the thought of this book that they definitely wanted to become part of it. They wanted to put their thinking and actions on paper in order to make this book more complete. Hey, what can I say about that. That's what friends are for. And of course, these friends also have experiences and have met people in their lives that have influenced them and therefore influenced this book. It seemed like a good idea to me to spread the thinking process wider this time than my mind only.

My friends Jason Fazackerley, Geerd Schlangen, Jeroen Verkuyl and Herman van Leeuwen started to work and became vital elements of this book. They brought their great experiences together and shared ideas and examples. To be honest, it took me some time to get them going with writing, but after they had started they did not seem to want to stop. What a passion and energy these guys threw into their chapters. Unbelievable. Where did their energy come from? Well, simple, their energy came from their passion for the topic. And besides that they are passionate believers that you can only build sustainable companies by doing. These guys are doers. Another great friend of mine, Dirk Jasper and his team, started to work as well. Dirk is the best designer in the world I know and he asked me one simple question. 'Does it have to be a prize winner again?' What he meant was that this book should not be a simple book like any book. This book should become a page turner as well as a totally different piece of work. The title of the book in some way has to be expressed in the design. The book has to be itself. My first book about creativity and entrepreneurship had to show these words in the design. For that reason the book became the first book on the marketplace that completely changed the design of a management-book. From boring to sexy.

The book became a combination of experiences, a combination of dreams, of opinions, of meetings, of the world.

And again the ambition of this book is that people start *doing* after having read it. That they start using the ideas that are written in it, that they visit the websites that are mentioned, that they implement projects in their company, that they spread the passion.

Because that's it; pick up the passion from this book, feel the passion. Take it away into your own organization and be successful. You know it's all about Passion and there is no other energy source that will keep you going.

Concluding; this book has to help you to ignite your passion. Sustainability @ the Speed of Passion.

by Joep Bertrams

'First they ignore you. Then they ridicule you. And then they attack you and want to burn you. And then they build monuments to you.' (Mahatma Ghandi)

WHY
AM I HERE?

→ Think about your personal role in life
→ Are people interested in sustainability at all?
→ What is your Passion?

The title of this first chapter is a very intriguing question. Why am I here is a difficult question to answer for many people. Why? Because they never think about it. People live their lives and quite often do not think too much about it. Although they think constantly, of course, because we cannot stop our brains from thinking. But sitting down in order to define the meaning of being is not so easy.

And even if you think about this question you will have to define what you mean by 'here' in 'why am I HERE'. What is here? The planet? The place I am physically in right now? My body? The company I work for? My country? My family? It can be anything and actually it doesn't matter very much. But when we want to answer the question on how to build a sustainable company it is important that you think about why you work for this company.

From my own experience I can say that building a company from scratch is by far the easiest. Of course there is nothing in the beginning of a start-up. So you start with no customers, no money and no employees etc. The big advantage is that you can build everything according to your own ideas. Which means that you can also select the people you want and need. You just select the people with the company values in their genes, believing in the mission as you do. That helps, it really does. No internal alignment programs to get everyone behind the promise. No work sessions to explain how to put the values in practice. Wow. Building a sustainable company is therefore more difficult in existing companies because there you start off with a group of people, the employees. You have a complete environment that you have inherited, with customers, shareholders, suppliers, employees, neighbors, the planet. We call that group 'the stakeholders'; the group of people that have an interest in the well-being of the company.

These stakeholders have different but also equal interests. Each stakeholder is interested in the long-term development of the company, because that means that he or she can profit from the company over the long term. Whether it is money or dividend for the shareholder, or being a well paying customer for the supplier, a good employer for the employee, a good caretaker for the planet etc. There are many interests the company has to serve. But the common denominator is 'long-term'. In general all economical theories talk about a 'going concern' when talking about a company. And a going concern is long-term. In theory, it never stops. This in itself is sustainability in its purest essence.

We want to create a company that serves its stakeholders indefinitely; a sustainable company, a company that can sustain, a company that can survive and will exist for generations, serving all its stakeholders well.

If you read and re-read the above you might think this is perfectly normal. It is normal behavior. It is the way you were probably raised by your parents as I was.

My mother always told me not to throw trash away on the street. 'Take it home with you and throw it in the garbage can,' she said. That is how I learned to take care of the planet in a very very small way. So, to me it also is normal behavior to drive a car that is not overly polluting the planet or not to use too much electricity. Take care of your own stuff and taking care of the planet is in essence the same. So, behave well and treat others as you would like to be treated yourself is normal principle.

In that respect one can imagine that the whole discussion about sustainability is a non-discussion about normal human behavior.

Indeed that would be true, were it not that apparently many people suddenly show different behavior when it comes to making money. Running a company seems to be something completely different for some people as to living a good life.

And yes, there are always plenty of reasons not to be able to live a good life in a company. 'We can only be profitable if such and such..', 'we cannot survive if we do such and such', 'we have to pay salaries', 'there is an economic crisis', are some of the reasons for people not to be sustainable.

One very confrontational question is the following; 'If you could hire the absolute best sales person on earth, but that person only wants to join the company if he/she can drive a big polluting car, what would you do?' Hire or not? Most companies would say 'Of course we hire, because we have to survive. And what difference does one car make?'

Mind you. Any idea how many companies there are in this world hiring this polluting short-term saleswonder?

Remember the question: 'Why am I here?'

Back to the statement I made earlier. Building a sustainable company is far easier when starting from scratch.

But most people reading this book do not start from scratch. They work in an environment that they want to turn into something with a long-term vision.

Well, let me surprise you then. Most employees probably will not be interested in your great and world-improving ideas. They have different things on their mind like their salaries, their colleagues, their dreams, vacations and families, children and many more. 'Cut the crap about your sustainable ideas and get back to work!' The biggest initial problem you have to solve is your own staff, that you have not hand-picked as you would in a start-up or in most family companies. You are stuck with your employees in a way. Or are you?

Experience tells us that at most 10% of all employees will respond enthusiastically about your ideas to turn the company into a sustainable environment. And as in any other change, the majority of people will wait and see. And then of course you always have the 10 to 20% of people who think your ideas are complete bull, but unfortunately they don't say that. They will just block and frustrate any steps you want to make on your way towards sustainability.

People even say 'Oh, I am getting sick of this sustainability-word.' Like it is a battle already won. Like we are already there; as if human behavior is already sustainable and companies really do have a long-term vision.

Come on, get a life, most people in this world have no single idea what sustainability really means. To most people in the world it is an intellectual luxury discussion that they don't want to be part of. And in reality, it is true. Most people in the world have other worries, like what will we eat tomorrow or how do we get water. Those are the problems of life. But does that then mean that this intellectual luxury discussion is nonsense and that we should not worry about building sustainable companies or that we should not worry in which CO_2-blurping car our sales-manager drives?

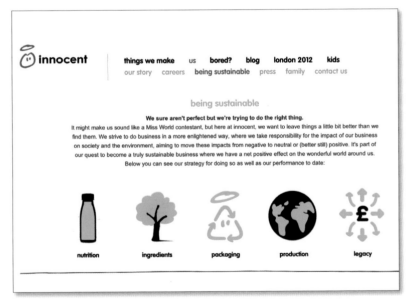

Well, Innocent certainly made a start.
www.innocentdrinks.co.uk/us/being-sustainable

No, it is my true belief that the people who care should make People who care
a beginning, no matter how small that beginning really is. should make a
We call it a water-drop on a hot plate; it disappears when beginning.
it hits the hot plate. It is a long-term commitment that
you make when you decide to turn your company into a sustainable
environment. And it is likely to become a hostile environment when
you are starting to touch the kernel that doesn't want to change.

A long-term journey

The first step is easy but very scary; present to your shareholders that
you are planning something like this. Talking, telling, presenting and
writing down are necessary initial steps to make. But you have to
realize that you are not actually doing anything in that phase.

Making moves that cut into the flesh are difficult ones. The first
steps towards carbon-neutrality are easy, but as soon as people really
have to get rid of their polluting cars it becomes difficult to move
forward. Many companies with visionary leaders, building sustainable
organizations, revert back to the old situation as soon as this visionary
leader leaves. That shows us how companies, and the people within
these companies, really think! As it shows that these leaders have left
before finishing their sustainable mission. As long as it's not in the
way of working and as long as it's not in people's DNA, a company isn't
really sustainable. Before it sinks in to all employees in a company,
one needs at least one generation. In our company we have started
a process of actively replacing people who did not share our dreams
and ideas about sustainability. That is an expensive process, I can tell
you. But I am certain that it will bring a better company for the future,
with better customers, better shareholders and better results.

There is no discussion that long-term oriented, sustainable companies give a better long-term result to the stakeholders of which
shareholders are one. But it is important to have that long-term
patience. Shareholders interested in short-term, quarterly-oriented,
gains are not supportive to building a sustainable environment. So,
maybe these shareholders shouldn't be yours either. More and more
'pockets of money', banks and private equity houses, are interested

in sustainable companies because the return on their investment is proven to be higher.

Keep pushing forward

Coming back to employees. The solution there is to take a long-term stance and keep pushing forward. There are no short-term gains, it is a culture change we are talking about here. And yes, if you speak with every employee individually, they will probably agree on your ideas, as long as it doesn't hinder them. Building a sustainable company is a long-term and extremely difficult process. Do not underestimate it. Do not see it as a short-term issue that you have to solve, like the many other business problems you have to tackle. It is a culture change we are talking about here and these processes take forever.

When reading the above you might lose most of the energy you need in building a sustainable company. This book however is meant to help you in a very pragmatic way in defining and taking steps to move forward. It is my opinion that you should act and talk as little as possible. Definitely in the beginning it is extremely important to show results and take action. In our company we started being a sustainable company by letting the employees define ten projects they thought would be helpful. Deliberately, we did not start with a definition phase and planning phase. We thought it would be better to begin first and think later. Of course that sounds dangerous, doesn't it. It is the only way to start the process, so we have learned. Act! Your first action? Answer the question.

Why are you here? That question is engraved in my head when I am being confronted with setbacks in the process of building a sustainable company. Because I realize that being sustainable starts with me. Starts with you!

I am here in this world with the responsibility to leave it behind in the same way (or even better) as I found it in when I was born. That is my responsibility and it is yours as well. With that belief in mind I am running companies and creating value for the stakeholders that are linked to it.

I have created and started twenty companies in my life. I have created and started twenty companies in my life.
And from every company I have learned many things. Slowly
but surely I am beginning to form an idea of how companies
should be run. I have no doubt made all the mistakes that
could be made in trying to be long-term oriented, but in all
instances the long-term orientation has helped me more
than short term hit-and-run actions. And I have also learned
to become realistic, hence the realistic approach and pragmatism
shown in this book. My advice? Stay grounded – it is useless to be a
theoretical visionary with your head in the cloud. If you really want
to build a sustainable company prepare yourself for all the problems
and criticism you'll face because you want to change your company
culture.

Sustainability consists of 3 P's. Profit, People and Planet. If the
company is not profitable, there is no company, there are no employees
and there are no stakeholders to serve. So, being profitable is the first
law of economics. Only when you have a profitable company you can
start to work on how you treat your people. That in itself is a very
delicate and detailed process. And only when your people are treated
well and feel well, can you really start to make a long-term impact on
the world. Only when all these conditions are right can you become
sustainable. I know, it is slow and it takes time, but you have to define
the building blocks for sustainability very carefully. It is a lifetime
project, but so are you.

Why are you here? Is a lifetime question that takes your whole life to
answer. You are here to contribute something and even knowing that
many people who do not care for sustainability for the right reasons
are also here for a reason.

We are here to contribute. That in itself creates an important
question that could just as easily have been the title of this chapter.
'What is your contribution?' Trying to define that is the second
fundamental question I am asking my employees. Start the process by
asking 'Why are you here' and start the process with yourself by asking
why you are here. I could not be with a company that does not care.
I could not work for a company or run a company that just doesn't
know why it exists, what its existential reason for being is. It would

not mean anything for me, and it would be a waste of time to spend my days with people who have no single clue why they are doing what they are doing. How could that be a passionate environment?

And yes, it is Passion with a capital P that should be the fourth P of sustainability, because without Passion there just would not be enough energy to perform the absolute difficult task of building a sustainable company.

So, go for sustainability, go for the four P's: Profit, People, Planet, Passion.

The new pioneers,
Tania Ellis, ISBN 978-0-470-74842-8

Out of the box,
Gunter Pauli, ISBN 1-920019-40-5

IIP Duurzame ICT, Strategic Research Agenda,
ISBN 978-90-817521-0-7

De Duurzaamheidsrevolutie,
Herman Verhagen, ISBN 978-80-6224-512-3

Leadership sustainability,
Michael Fullan, ISBN 0-7619-3873-7

Rip Off Your Necktie and Dance,
Leen Zevenbergen, ISBN 978-1906403690

Confessions of a radical industrialist,
Ray Anderson, ISBN 978-1-847-94029-2

Biomimicry,
Janine Benyus, ISBN 978-0-06-053322-9

WHAT TO DO NOW?

① Ask all the employees the question 'Why are you here?'

② Let them answer it in some short sentences

③ Share these answers with your colleagues

④ Ask every employee to write down his or her 4 passions

⑤ Share these hobbies on a website, like theprideofqurius.nl

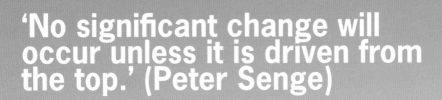

'No significant change will occur unless it is driven from the top.' (Peter Senge)

WE NEED A NEW ORDER

CHAPTER 2

→ Everybody is being controlled
→ Improving instead of repairing
→ Turning the pyramid upside down

Definitely, we are entering a new world. A world that needs a new order. That needs some perspective on what's currently going on.

Having a so-called helicopter view is an absolute must. When you look at the world from outer space what you see is a beautiful thing. But the closer you get, the more ugly and problematic things appear. When you get in detail into the Amazon rainforest you see that astonishingly large areas of forest are disappearing every day. But also in Indonesia large areas of rainforest have been cut down. When you fly in an airplane the damage being done every day makes you sick in your stomach. When you walk around in the devastated areas you panic.

The same is true when you look at companies, at organizations. Surrounded by enormous amounts of rules and regulations we are trying to survive crisis after crisis.

Over past years, between 1980 and 2004, in The Netherlands the amount of laws has grown by 60%. In Europe, the number of regulatory institutions has grown heavily. Every sector has a control organization with which we try to control what is going on. And of course we need authorities that also keep an eye on these control institutions.

An ever-growing part of the working population is occupied with controlling others. This system wants to tell us something. The system wants to tell us that we do not need to worry. Everything is under control. But we are of course fooling ourselves. The system we are building only offers a fake security that doesn't help us, but brings us closer to the end. The system is killing itself.

In a micro-way we see the same within organizations. Large and public organizations are having major problems in sticking to the rules. And the rules that apply for large public companies are the same for small public companies. There are so many rules and regulations that the cost of applying them is devastating. And also the time that is being consumed with sticking to the rules is absolutely ridiculous.

Organizations normally have Boards that have to control them. But these Boards are controlled and regulated as well, so they all search for security. They search for security that nothing can go wrong.

But the secret of entrepreneurship is that you can never be sure of success. Always something can go wrong. For example, nobody foresaw the plunge in share-prices that hit the global economy in July of 2011.

Many companies saw a decline in their value of more than 50%. These companies stayed the same, produced the same products, still had the same customers and the same employees. And yet, from one week to the other, the value of these companies was cut in half. On what then is the value of these companies based, one can wonder?

Is it based on economic value? On value of revenue? Or on intrinsic value? With my background as an economist, I know there are many ways to value a company. But I also know that, where many years ago the value of shares was based upon profit divided by the number of shares, it currently has nothing to do with the economic performance of the company anymore. Stock markets are based upon emotions. And the emotions of the general public are based upon negative sentiment. Why is that? Because all the news that the general audience gets is negatively biased! And why is that? Because the general audience is interested in negative news and the press knows it, so that explains the bias.

The above has been researched in great detail and it is quite alarming that we have a negative bias in the world that surrounds us. And more and more we are trying to protect ourselves against these negative influences.

Stock markets are based upon emotions.

In the beginning of 2012 we saw that there had been a global build-up of a financial crisis. Nobody knows exactly what the impact will be on economies or the companies that form these economies.

Let's keep it simple

The basic elements of national economies are companies, small and large. It is they who generate the money to keep the economy going. With the money generated by companies, salaries can be paid and taxes can be paid, which in turn supplies money for governments who can then employ other people and pay them. This mechanism is simple when you look at it from a great distance (as I explained earlier). The closer you get to it of course the more complex it gets. Some people have a gift of making things simple and some people have a gift to do the contrary; indeed making things more complex. It is a fact that there are more people able to make things complex than people making things simple. The truth is that one needs a much higher intelligence to make complex things simple.

But let's try to make it simple now. There is not so much wrong with the economy as the world turns. People live, eat, sleep and work. From a macro economic perspective the population of the world grows, along with the need for food, shelter, work etc. This calls for growth as long as we can supply it.

Still, because of mistakes made by both financial institutions (who also wanted to behave as if they were entrepreneurs) and governments (who failed to stick to the rules they agreed on) the normal companies are suffering. Suffering, not because the markets are not there, but suffering because we are putting more and more control mechanisms on our financial institutions. And we treat all financial institutions the same way of course. Big or small, we are trying to get a tight control over our financial institutions, creating layer upon layer of control mechanisms. Hoping to insure ourselves against possible disasters.

And that as well is a fake security, just as we have seen many more fake securities being created year after year, generation after generation. Because we are creating an economy that is blocked like arteries that are being cluttered with fat. Slowly but surely the blood stops flowing and the brain does not get oxygen anymore.

Does nobody see how we are killing the economy? Does nobody see how we are killing the entrepreneurship that is necessary to survive, companies and countries alike? Does nobody see that the less intelligent people are creating difficult solutions out of simple ones? As mentioned before, one needs intelligent people to create simple solutions to complex problems. But now they are throwing control mechanism after control mechanism towards a problem when they don't even know exactly what the problem is.

Because, if the problem would only be that financial liquidity is needed to keep the already healthy economy flowing, we would need exactly the opposite solution to the financial problems than we currently are creating.

Now we are going to take one step deeper into the economics system, we are going to enter corporations and companies. We are going to look inside the mechanisms that create our wealth in order to see if the economic laws and happenings are the same on the inside as well as outside. Are we also killing our companies inside? Are we also building mechanisms inside that hinder our people from becoming happy in their work? We have seen that the People-element is crucial in building sustainable organizations, inside a sustainable society.

We have seen before that we are working very hard to build the most unsustainable environment for ourselves, but it is now important to see what is happening at the smallest micro level – the individual employee. Besides the fact that it is interesting to see what happens there and what we can do about it, it is also interesting to realize that these same individual workers play an essential role in the construction of society. What is the attitude of the individual worker towards the organization they are in? Are they proud to be there? Do they love their colleagues (not all of them)? Are they motivated?

Well, I don't know. One needs to be pretty strong and a little bit intelligent to be able to understand and value all the news that is given to us on a continuous basis. People are bombarded on a continuous basis with news. At least they think it is news, because that is what the producers of that news want us to think. And since it has been proven that news is biased negatively and that we never seem to be able to know for sure if we are reading and seeing the truth (particularly because of the internet, which devalues all news into one big grey mediocre blurp) one has to be pretty strong to stay positive.

People in general have a vision of the future, which is much less positive than they did ten years ago. And this vision seems to be worsening.

And I have to admit that we indeed are facing some grave challenges.

In our wish to improve our macro and micro economic systems we are always using the current systems as the starting point. In that respect we are, and have always been, repairing the system and we have not been improving, as stated by Herman Verhagen in his book about the Sustainability revolution.

Both in our macro and micro systems we need to make a new start, we need to innovate. And this innovation in my view has to start with the individual. Individuals together form companies, but at the same time they form society. And individuals are seeking a good life in general. Knowing that mechanism and using it to our advantage can be the catalyst to change both companies and societies in a fundamental way. Most people that I have spoken to about re-building society into a sustainable one and doing the same for companies agree upon one thing. And that one thing is very fundamental. It is the absolute necessity that leaders are driving the change.

In improving and innovating, the highest step on the ladder is organizational innovation. This is often forgotten because most of the time if people are thinking about innovation they are thinking about product innovation. But sustainable change needs innovation of the organization. This kind of difficult change takes more time and is also longer lasting. Yes, it is sustainable.

Going back to the individual elements of society and organizations; that's where the starting point should be.

And do not underestimate the passion element here, because people are driven and get their energy by their own passion. If a leader gives a passionate speech one can feel it in their stomach. You can see the shiny eyes when people are passionate; they start to glow. Everybody knows the process of dreaming and the good feeling that that creates.

Passionately building a vision from the top is a very difficult first step to make. Because it has to happen with that one person at the top. Or it has to happen with the people who appoint the top individual.

If this person at the top starts with turning the old fashioned corporate pyramid upside-down, we are getting in the winning mode. Because the individual people, with their individual dreams and ambitions, will make sure it will all happen. This is my absolute and optimistic view.

Research in Western societies has shown that 17-18% of all working people do not want to work for organizations that do not want to align to social responsibility. And the surprise I have for you is that these people are the most talented and intelligent ones. These 17-18% are exactly the people you want to employ. These are exactly the people that will differentiate your company from others. These people are the innovative ones. I can go on and on about this, but the picture seems clear to me. And simple after all.

Start at the bottom
We start at the bottom and stimulate people to change. Without doubt, people want to change. But we have to give them a good reason. And that reason needs to be given to them by their leader(s). Ray Anderson of Interface found a reason.

He stimulated his organization with good reasons to change and become sustainable, become responsible, become different. Thirty years ago Ray Anderson felt ashamed and knew he was destroying the world with the company he founded, *Interface* **FLOR**® Interface. He felt so ashamed that he announced a change towards sustainability that nobody understood. I can imagine that his employees and other stakeholders at that moment must have thought that he had gone crazy. Ray had a big advantage though; Interface was his company. More or less he could do with it what he wanted. But over the past decades he worked vigorously to change Interface and implement his sustainable vision to all levels. I am saying TO ALL LEVELS.

That is what I would call leadership. Create a vision and implement it. Never give up, because your vision is you. You cannot live without this vision.

The key to involving and including the people of your organization in this vision is that it has to inspire them. People have to want to belong to the group that fights for this vision.

Leaders are no longer masters who instruct their slaves. No, leaders are people who inspire their fellow citizens, so to speak.

In inspiring individual employees one creates a community. I have heard people use the word sect. In this connotation that is not so bad. We create a group of inspired people who feel the same and have the same ambitions.

Turn the pyramid upside down. In old fashioned organizational models often a pyramid is used in representing the shape of the organization. One leader at the top, who has ten people (we call this a span of control) reporting to him/her and they again have their teams and so on. This is a very pragmatic way of representing an organization, but it has many elements in it that make it ultimately unworkable. People all want to climb the ladder of the pyramid in order to become the boss, make more money, impress their partners and neighbors, make their parents happy and many other reasons.

People who love their profession and develop themselves into experienced colleagues often do not climb this corporate ladder and get frustrated. Is experience no longer important?

By turning the pyramid upside down one shows the fact that the leaders are now the lowest in rank, supporting their organization. And that servant leadership is exactly the kind of leadership needed to build a sustainable organization. This servant leader helps his team, his employees, to discover their passions and bring these in line with the overall passion in building a new organization.

If you would now ask me to paint the exact path forward here I will have to disappoint you. Because there are hardly any good examples of organizations who have gone the whole way. There are some, yes, and there are even some organizations that have started a very long time ago, 25 or 30 years, to make this fundamental change. Companies like Semco, Interface, Ben&Jerry's and others started early on. They even formed an organization that was the world pioneer in changing organizations around. This group was called Social Venture Network. Founded around 1987 in the United States, it has always been a platform for sustainable organizations. My advice is to go there to learn from them and learn from their experiences.

So, the leaders of this time are entering a difficult path with no defined outcome and it takes a long time to get it done (if ever). And I am certain that when organizations are being turned around, organizations being the energy that keeps the world turning, the individuals within those organizations will turn societies around as well.

The way that we are going forward now is a dead end street and too many people are beginning to see that now.

1. Start with the Vision; write down your long-term goals

3. Start presenting the Vision of the company

2. Become a leader or involve the leaders

STEPS TO CHANGE

Create a sect

7. Repeat the message and keep repeating, over and over!

5. Form teams within the company to support this long-term Vision

6. Start small projects to change

4. Ask every colleague the question Are you in or out?

'THIS IS A LONG-TERM JOURNEY'

MARIJKE MARS
(Global Vice President Sustainability, Petcare Division)

Interviewing Marijke Mars of Mars Inc was an inspiring experience. It stressed some basic and important issues that are of great importance to companies willing to become sustainable. Some very strong and interesting principles. Before we spoke about the 5 Principles of Mars there were some issues that struck me and that I would like to mention first.

At Mars there are no employees, but Associates. What a great way to stress the importance of the People element. There are 65,000 Associates, working in a global organization that is run on the basis of 5 simple and straightforward Principles.

Another thing that struck me was that the company is very market-driven, wants to win and wants to make a profit. The governance culture is extremely strong and there is a huge performance driven culture, which shows the fine line that exists between the soft sustainability and the hard profit. Without profit, there is no sustainability because there is no company.

Finally and almost of the highest importance, Marijke stressed the fact that Passion for building a sustainable company is easier to reach when speaking about how to create a better world than how to get cost savings. The word Passion is important and during our whole conversation I could feel both the Passion for the company as well as the Passion for the sustainable approach. Marijke mentioned that 'it is his Passion', when talking about how the CEO of Mars thinks about sustainability.

That's why the title of this book is 'Sustainability @ the Speed of Passion'. We always speak about the three P's when we define sustainability, and we are inclined to forget the most important and vital P, being Passion. Without Passion in the top and with all employees/ Associates there is no real sustainability.

The long journey at Mars started decades ago. The family-based company, which Mars is, started working on a value system in the 40's. Marijke's grandfather implemented a consumer oriented value system that eventually resulted in the 5 Principles that are guiding the company nowadays. These 5 Principles are Quality, Responsibility, Mutuality, Efficiency and Freedom. On the basis of these principles a more organized sustainability program started in 2007. That program was defined for a period of at least 30 years, with long-term goals in 2040.

The reason for this long period is that one generation lasts about 30 years, so the realistic timeframe for results is one generation. What did I tell you about a long-term approach?

Of course you can go to www.mars.com and read much more about the principles, but Marijke gave a brief overview of them as well. The customer, the consumer in Mars' case, is of the highest importance. Therefore, giving quality to that customer is of the highest importance. Without quality it would be impossible to build a long-term relationship with the consumer. This Principle is logically followed by the next one; Responsibility. Everybody has his or her role to play and has to take up the responsibility that belongs to it. Step up when you see an opportunity or when you see something wrong. Take action and never blame others.

The third Principle is Mutuality. Mutuality between all parties, like suppliers and Mars, or consumers and Mars, is essential. In any long-term approach it can never be a one way street. It always has to go two ways. Mutually beneficial solutions are the basis for any long-term approach and for any sustainable approach.

The Fourth Principle is Efficiency; waste nothing and use everything to the full. This is very important when talking about resources, human as well as product. And finally and most logically the fifth Principle is Freedom. While one would think that the final one is very philosophical it is actually very pragmatic. By freedom the company means financial freedom. When financially free, a company can move in each direction it wishes, can become a meaningful player in society.

Talking a little bit more about this financial freedom, Marijke mentioned the fact that companies, just by being there, already play a very important role in society. In terms of sustainability, it is often mentioned that companies should donate to society or in some way 'give something back'. But we should never forget that, by just being there, companies already give much to society. What would you think about all the taxes that are being paid and the jobs that are created. Indeed, taxes and jobs are the elements that whole societies are based upon, and often they are just taken for granted.

Within Mars, the Associates play an important role in the sustainability program. Not only are they working according to the five Principles, but also they share best practices, they communicate about it, they are acting as ambassadors throughout the company. Mars is providing its Associates with the means to actually DO things, like time to organize a Green Day or help with a carbon-minimizing car policy.

To Mars, sustainability seems to be a way of life, which it should be. With both a long term (30 years), medium term as well as a short term plan (harvesting the low hanging fruit) the company sets an example of how to be a responsible player in society.

♥ world
mproving
Entrepreneur

My friend Engbert Breuker came up with the WIE idea. I like it!

'There are some people who live in a dream world, and there are some who face reality; and then there are those who turn one into the other.' (Douglas Everett)

BUILDING A SUSTAINABLE TEAM

→ The world is changing
→ Myths we have to face
→ Dreamers and Realists

The Western world has seen a massive shift over the last few centuries. The Industrial Revolution of the 18th and 19th century saw unparalleled change as the populations of many countries shifted from unmechanized manual labor and subsistence farming, where a family basically grew enough food to feed themselves, to an era of machine agriculture and manufacturing. During this change the world's average per capita income increased tenfold whilst the world population increased six-fold.

Over most of this period people were pretty much born into a job; the son of a blacksmith would have become a blacksmith; children would work the land farmed by their parents and grandparents. As the industrial revolution gained momentum the population, except for the very privileged few, would follow their parents into the cotton mill, or docks or coal mine. Basically, you would work within walking distance of where you were born. But as this was happening a sudden change began as new skills were required. The industrial revolution created opportunities for traders, managers, designers, engineers and entrepreneurs. This is when society began to really value education, which became a necessity if we were to continue to advance; as a minimum, workers needed to be able to read, write and add-up. Employers began to support education, many actually financing the building and running of schools. In most cases this was not a philanthropic gesture but a means to an end. Many of our parents and grandparents had very few jobs in their lifetime. A large percentage only had one job, except for the occasional interruption of a war, when they would serve their country. Because of this, employers were keen to educate new workers through schemes such as apprenticeships – investment in people was considered safe. It is really only in the last 50 years that the workforce has become mobile, and increasingly so. In the USA it is predicted that current learners will have had 10 to 14 jobs just by the age of 38! This makes the logic of investing in your employees questionable as the return on that investment is no longer apparent.

20 years ago we did not have the internet. 10 years ago we did not have social media. Change is happening with increasing velocity. In high-value societies many of the top in-demand jobs did not exist just a few years ago. If an undergraduate enters university today, half of what they learn in their first year will be out of date before they graduate. The technologies they will work with have not been invented, and we don't yet know what problems they will have to solve.

Pre-Industrial Revolution, in the days of subsistence farming, we had a sustainable workforce. In fact, you could argue that those days defined sustainability itself. Through most of the industrial revolution the lack of mobility meant most people had a job for life and few aspirations to move onwards or upwards.

Dispel the myths

Given that we have an increasingly mobile workforce and an ever increasing need for learning throughout out working lives how can we create a sustainable team? Is it possible or affordable? We have to accept that there are some things that we cannot alter – the velocity of change being one of them. But, there are some myths that should be challenged and dispelled if we are to create a sustainable team to power our sustainable business and sustainable world:

If you train your staff they will leave to join your competitors: People do not leave a business because they are suddenly more marketable, they leave because they are not satisfied. In many cases they should leave. Let them go if they are not happy, not part of the team. Good people managers are close enough to their team to know if someone is not satisfied. If an employee is not happy, and the issues cannot be fixed, then why would you invest in their training and development – in their mind they have already left. And if they take with them skills that you have helped them develop then that is not a bad thing, they are taking them into the greater society where they will create success. Sometimes, employees are dissatisfied because training and career development is what they desire – so give it, it will satisfy them and they will reward you through effort and commitment.

Only with the best people you get the best team: It would often be advised that you should recruit the best people you can get, and if you cannot afford the best, but you consider they will be instrumental in your future success then you should find other ways to entice those individuals to your business, perhaps through shared ownership or some other self-funding reward based on success. But, there is a 'But'; employing the best individuals does not make the best team. This is commonly seen in sport, where the best players from the most successful teams in a national league are picked to represent their country internationally. The national team does not necessarily perform to expectation because the best individual players do not always compliment the rest of the team. When recruiting one should look at the team just as closely as the individual.

If I taught you everything I knew, the company wouldn't need me: I was recently talking with a friend who had been approaching the end of his working life when he suffered a bad car accident. He may never work again. This friend has some rare skills and experience. He is a carpenter and is able to repair and restore old furniture using the same skills he learnt as a boy – skills that are not taught today in any educational establishment. He used tools that a young carpenter would not recognize, let alone know how to use. I was surprised when he told me that his biggest regret was not that he'd had this awful life altering accident, or that he may not be able to work again. His biggest regret was that he had not had the opportunity to pass his skills on to someone younger, he had tears in his eyes when he told me this. His talent would be taken to the grave. Whilst we recognizse the exponential rate of change, we must not forget that many skills and requirements really don't change or change very slowly. Much of the knowledge I gained at university twenty something years ago is still relevant today. Whilst it is true that most of us like to learn new skills, it is often far more rewarding to pass knowledge and experience on. A sustainable team is one where experience and knowledge is shared, passed down. As we get older and wiser what could be more rewarding than helping younger people to benefit from our experience, and what a crime it is when talent is lost.

Never go back: I was fortunate enough to work with a large global computer manufacturer whilst studying, gaining good experience during vacation from university. I was grateful for the experience they gave me and for the financial support during my studies. This organization, like many, made it very clear that they expected 100% loyalty and if an employee were to leave to join another organization, competitor or not, they would never be able to return. On graduation I was offered a job with this company and it was made obvious that this was my once in a lifetime opportunity to join. If I didn't, then I would never be offered a job with them again. I thought hard, but decided to take a position in a small dynamic organization. Ego often gets in the way of doing good business and there is no room for this weakness in a true team. If a company has an ego then it is limiting itself by keeping unhappy people on the books and disregarding those who have left and, perhaps gained some fantastic experience working for its competitors, from returning.

Training is expensive: Right, but what is the cost of ignorance? The training industry has become quite commoditized over the years, which is to its detriment. Two costs can be applied to training; the first is the tangible cost paid to the training organization, the second, and most important, is the investment of having that individual released from the business for the period of the training. The quality of a training course obviously has a direct impact on the skills of the trainee, but poor quality training, where perhaps the pace of the course is aimed at the (s)lowest denominator, can be quite demotivating; the trainee begins to wish they were still at work, contributing. Training is such an important part of ensuring that the team has the skills needed, and that they are not over-reliant on one or two team members. The highest quality of training ensures that you maximize the return on investment and can highly motivate individuals to apply their new skills and excel in their job. Always invest in the best training you can get.

So much for the myths to be dispelled when you want to build a sustainable team. But this chapter wouldn't be complete without the wisdom of Cameron. I know, it is not often in a book like this that you would come across a quote from a fictional character, especially one from the American comedy TV show Modern Family, but at least it is Barack Obama's favourite family viewing and I think the quote from the character Cameron is so important to building a sustainable business:

'There are dreamers, and there are realists in this world. You'd think dreamers would find dreamers, and realists would find realists, but more often than not, the opposite is true.
You see, dreamers need the realists to keep them from soaring too close to the sun. And the realists? Well, without the dreamers, they may never get off the ground.'

This is so true – the world is full of examples of dreamers and visionaries who have been successful by recognizing that they need to surround themselves with realists. Often it is the dreamer who appears to lead successful businesses, but that is often the perception of the public eye. Steve Jobs was not the founder of Apple Inc, he was the co-founder with Ronald Wayne (who left soon after) and Steve Wozniak, a computer engineer and programmer. Rolls Royce Limited was founded in 1914 by Charles Stewart Rolls and Henry Royce. Henry was the steady, time-served engineer whereas Charles was the dreamer who at the age of just 32 was the first Briton to be killed in a flying accident.

When building a sustainable team it is important to get the right balance of dreamers and realists. If the balance is not right then the venture will either not get off the ground or it could end up being a costly disaster. It is not difficult to measure the balance in an existing team – and generally teams have a natural ability to form the right balance subconsciously as opposites do attract. But this should be tested, and if a new team is to be conceived then some careful selection should be done.

Review how your business contributes to the development of current and future employees.

Employ the best people you can, but more importantly build the best team you can; **identify** the dreamers and the realists.

Create a culture of continuous learners and teachers, and remember that you will be employing people for job roles that don't yet exist.

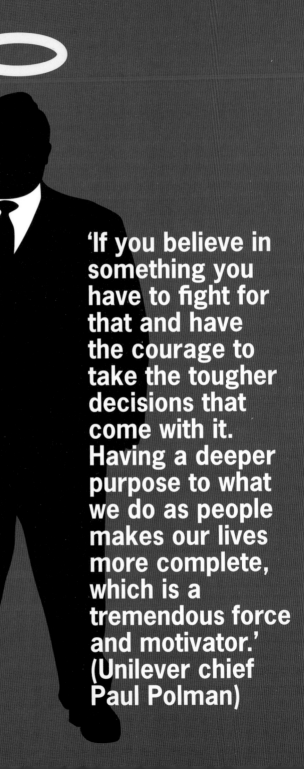

'If you believe in something you have to fight for that and have the courage to take the tougher decisions that come with it. Having a deeper purpose to what we do as people makes our lives more complete, which is a tremendous force and motivator.' (Unilever chief Paul Polman)

BECOME A WORLD-IMPROVING ENTREPRENEUR

→ Doing good is for all times
→ Starting from scratch or improving what's there?
→ Follow your heart is the best
→ Choose your eco-system

World-Improving Entrepreneurs: Doing good – where does it come from? We live in interesting and hopeful times. While some people are 'getting sick of the sustainability word', more and more care about what they can contribute to a better, more sustainable world. Through their work, through their behavior as a consumer and through their contribution to all kinds of citizen initiatives. Doing good is for all ages and it is a positive aspect of the human condition. Sometimes this social and responsible behavior seems to slip away. In difficult and harsh times like famines or wars it is mostly everybody for themselves, although there are always brave and social saints. Similarly, in times of growing wealth people are greedy and strive for more and more at the cost of underprivileged people and the environment. This creates unstable imbalances in wealth and health between social groups and geographies by polluting and disrupting nature and in the destruction of coherent societies through total individualization.

Since World War II the world has run a race of mass consumption, fuelled by the thirst for oil and driven by technology. Nobody seemed to care as long as it was in the name of progress. But somewhere in this enormous economic upswing there were people that stood up. The Club of Rome in 1972 and others raised the flag for the environment and many others stood up to fight social and economic imbalance.

Change starts with a mission

This responsibility can be traced back to all the leaders who improved the living conditions and positions of the poor proletariat, racial groups and even women. If we look back on the history of the 20th century many among us are inspired by the really legendary stories of Mahatma Gandhi, Martin Luther King and Nelson Mandela. They all accomplished the impossible mission they embodied, the cause they believed and lived for was driving them relentlessly. These significant examples inspire me in my continuous optimism: if you have a good and just mission, you can do it. Particularly when it is on a much smaller scale than all the iconic heroes.

But it is not only the 'big' personalities who form a source of inspiration. Personally I take a special interest in all the tens of thousands (or more) entrepreneurs in this world who have a world-improving mission with their company. Some of them do this by heritage or by nature. They learned from their parents to conduct a sustainable way of living. You can see some impressive examples from people and tribes living close to nature. They know as no one else their dependency on the ecosystem around them. So they have made balanced living a part of their ecosystem. And then there are people that have a specific character or a personal view on the world that almost automatically drives them towards doing good. They are fully authentic in what they do. They never thought of changing their lives, they live their lives and are passionate about the things they do.

A good example is probably Jamie Oliver who is passionate about cooking and is pulling more and more people into the fun of preparing tasty food. And with this positive energy he is including young urban rascals so they can learn a skill. And his passion gave him the authority to develop a program for healthy school meals in the UK and actually drive the program. And it is a worthwhile cause: the UK has the highest rate of childhood obesity in Europe, with 25% of young people being classified as obese or overweight.

There's a WIE in everyone

If you are not a saint or a world-improving entrepreneur by birth, there must be something on your path that makes you decide to become a World-Improving Entrepreneur. It could be that you are already an entrepreneur, reasonably successful and that you decide to change your business model. Step by step or radically. You can decide to make your business more compliant with the environment (greening-up). This is relatively easy: cleaner cars, less travelling, decrease energy use in facilities and processes, recycling etc. One step further: deliver products or services that improve the quality of the environment. This is the fun part. Here you start innovations and you are showing that you are a real entrepreneur. Socially, you can just comply and be a good citizen obeying the law and help when you are asked; or you can decide to drive change and pay respect, restore justice and offer people the fair opportunities to have a life where they can drive their own destiny as far as they are able to. Social innovations are not about pampering people but about building an inclusive society. If you are in a privileged position you can decide what you can do for others. It is just that easy. Whether you are a plumber, a lawyer, a systems engineer or Bill Gates.

Two types of WIE's: starting from scratch or making a turn. The hundreds of World-Improving Entrepreneurs who I have met over the last 20 years all had different approaches to their actual mission. Back in the '80's and '90's there were only a few entrepreneurs who started their business with a social ideal. Sometimes this was amateuristic and even charmingly naive. They were good people who just started without thinking too much. If you trace back the early days of the Body Shop and Ben & Jerry's ice-cream you'll find out that they started with very small ventures for no reason other than the challenge of starting it. Anita Roddick was inspired by a visit to the Berkeley Body Shop. This shop in Berkeley, California only used natural ingredients and helped to employ and train immigrant women. Roddick purchased the naming rights and started her Body Shop empire with just a little shop where she sold her 'fair trade and purely natural' body care products.

Ben Cohen & Jerry Greenfield were just two hippies that chanced upon an old milk factory in Vermont and decided out of the blue to start an ice cream company. It is amazing to see what grew out of these innocent seeds. In the beginning there was at the most a belief, a feeling or like Ben & Jerry's it was almost a joke. Once in the nineties when Ben & Jerry's was introduced in Europe by another WIE (the late Eckart J. Wintzen, founder of Origin, now ATOS it-services), the two of them gave a lecture at the Nijenrode Business University in The Netherlands. They explained that they met in high-school, where they were always lagging way behind their classmates during athletics classes. They became friends and during one of their trips to the sparkling environment of Vermont they decided to stay and make a living, brewing ice-cream. They loved the stuff themselves and thought it was worth trying to start a business even though they didn't really know anything about the finer details of the ice-cream business. But they did know about having fun and being inventive. What they did know though is that you need milk and there was plenty of it with all the farmers in the neighbourhood. These farmers were their first allies. Their first marketing campaign was smart and effective. In one word: bumper stickers!

All visitors that bought ice cream from the doorstep of their charming factory got a bumper sticker on their car: Ben & Jerry's Ice Cream. That is how the Vermont market was conquered. And once they had found out that you could earn money in making ice cream, while having fun and acting honest and fair, it became the magic mix of their company. And not even knowing it at that time they were WIE's. The rest is history and now that Ben & Jerry's is incorporated into food multinational Unilever, it is very much a brand with a mission. It certainly has infected the minds at Unilever, because now this global food company is geared to a full sustainable mission lead by its CEO Paul Polman.

So the good news is that you can just follow your heart (which is always the best) and start something you like. A gym, a flower shop, a paper company, a travel agency, a sock company, a coffee company, whatever comes to your mind and heart. You can be a WIE on a local, regional, national or global scale.

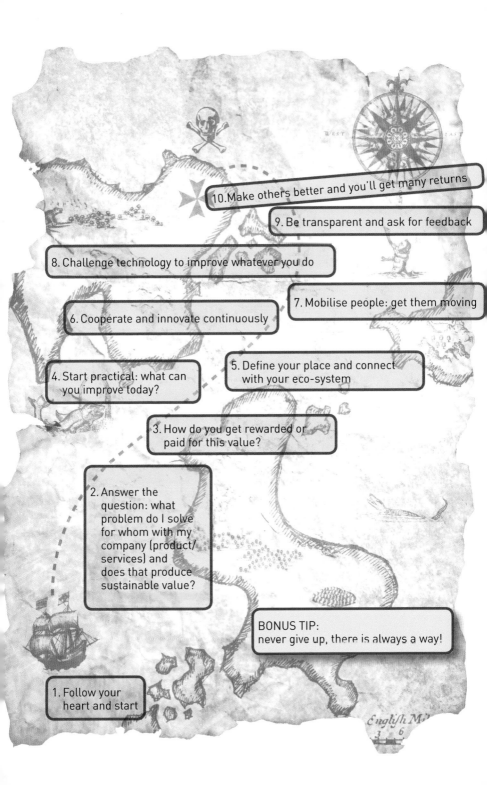

10. Make others better and you'll get many returns

9. Be transparent and ask for feedback

8. Challenge technology to improve whatever you do

7. Mobilise people: get them moving

6. Cooperate and innovate continuously

5. Define your place and connect with your eco-system

4. Start practical: what can you improve today?

3. How do you get rewarded or paid for this value?

2. Answer the question: what problem do I solve for whom with my company (product/services) and does that produce sustainable value?

BONUS TIP:
never give up, there is always a way!

1. Follow your heart and start

English M.
3   6

A CHANCE ENCOUNTER

GILES WHITELEY
SWR (Specialist Waste Recycling)

INTERVIEW

In 2007 Giles Whiteley boarded the over-night sleeper train from Inverness in Scotland to return to his London home following a weekend visiting his then girlfriend's parents. What started off as a normal train journey for Giles quickly turned into quite an adventure. On entering the bar on the train Giles found himself in conversation with a complete stranger. By the time they arrived in London a plan had developed. The unknown gentleman was Angus MacDonald, a serial entrepreneur, who had just become the owner of semi-distressed business Oakside

Environmental. Angus had been keen to enter into the environmental market and he had identified that Oakside had some great ideas but was struggling to successfully execute them. From that chance meeting on the sleeper train from Scotland, Angus appointed Giles as Chief Operating Officer, and then set about raising the investment required to put the company on solid foundations. Giles immediately set about securing the business and then growing it whilst capitalizing on those good ideas. The company Specialist Waste Recycling (SWR) was founded.

I arranged to meet Giles in a local London pub one evening after work to interview him for this book. I had met him many times previously, but that had been in a business setting where he would listen intently to everyone in the meetings and occasionally offer impressive foresight. What struck me when it was just the two of us talking over a pint of beer was that he just could not stop talking; his enthusiasm was outstanding and his passion infectious. Before we started talking about the business he had to tell me that when he joined SWR he drove a Range Rover with 250 thousand kilometres on the clock. He had calculated the environmental impact including the Embodied energy and end-of-life cost compared with the low mileage that he drove. It proved a better environmental case than the company's fleet of new Hybrid cars. In fact, he now wishes they hadn't invested in the Hybrids, because efficient diesel engine cars can give better fuel economy and don't contain all the batteries and embodied carbon found in the Hybrids (certainly those of 2007). Since joining SWR he has sold the Range Rover and now drives a Porsche – this of course is not the car of choice for your committed tree-hugger. But he explained, "...the car is kept at the office. I don't use it very much because I commute to the office by public transport." His Porsche is his luxury, but again it is a second hand model – "somebody else took the hit on the embodied energy", he argued.

Giles is very direct, and he talks at the speed of light. It took a little to get him to tell me about the business, I was keen to understand why he and Angus hit it off in such unique circumstances, and what about the great ideas that excited them both enough to commit their lives to SWR.

Traditional big companies could not serve all the automotive industry's needs. SWR manage the collection of up to 16 different waste streams. Traditional waste companies, including the big ones, need efficient routes, as they are primarily logistics organisations. The modus operandi of SWR is to find sectors that traditional companies do not serve well and then offer a better alternative in terms of customer care, service delivery and flexibility, primarily by delivering a mix of the best local contractors and utilising their own fleet for more niche waste types. Automotive was just the start. They are now building success stories in other sectors such as hospitality, builders merchants etc.

Angus and Giles like to challenge the status quo. In fact, I got the impression Giles likes to stick two fingers up at some traditionalists. "Traditional waste management companies have an estate of landfill sites that they need to fill or sorting facilities and furnaces that they need to feed. They have hundreds of trucks that they have to conjure up efficient routes for. This can mean that customers can be sold what is best for the waste company and not always the best solution for them. SWR has built a business where it runs very few vehicles, even though they move waste and recycling materials from A to B. Giles prefers to contract out the transport to best placed local transport providers. This allows him to put the right service mix together for each customer and not worry about getting the maximum number of journeys out of a vehicle. By utilising the vehicles of other firms who benefit from efficiencies of the work, he minimises the trucks he puts on the road; a carbon and cost win-win.

In 2011 SWR acquired another company, Smash & Grab. Again, this was a company that had a great idea, but was unable to exploit it. Smash & Grab designed and built a compact glass crushing machine. It can easily be installed in the back of house areas in bars or restaurants.

The operator loads it with glass bottles which it duly crushes and the crushed material passes down into a receptacle that can easily be emptied into the bin at the back of the premises. 80% of a bottle is air. The net effect of this equipment is that it takes the air out of the bottle, which means that much more glass material can be put in a bin before it needs to be emptied, which in turn means that instead of the bin being emptied daily, it may only need servicing twice per week. The customer is happy because they pay for fewer bin empties and therefore reduce the carbon footprint.

The reason Smash & Grab previously was not successful was because they could not sell enough units – they were too expensive for many establishments. Where Angus and Giles have been really clever is by not selling them. "Giles, you have confused me now", I said, and decided to get him another pint of beer. He explained, again with a great deal of passion, that the price objection from the customers was too great. By buying the company they could have the machines for the cost of manufacture. "So we give them away where they will provide a benefit" in return for the entire waste contract – glass included. SWR charge the customer less than they paid previously, provide a very practical solution and reduce CO_2 output.

Spending an evening with Giles was a pleasure. His energy and enthusiasm is truly infectious. The ambition, along with entrepreneurial spirit from Angus, to build a business that generates profit whilst creating a significant impact on CO_2 output is envied, maybe even by those traditional monolithic businesses.

'Knowing is not enough; we must apply. Willing is not enough; we must do.' (Johann Wolfgang von Goethe)

SUSTAINABLE RIGHT FROM THE START

→ Sustainability drives innovation
→ The idea is the strongest driver
→ Passion combined with focus
→ Motivation is their mojo
→ Understanding the impact makes you motivated
→ Excellent products make an excellent story

There are entrepreneurs who started their careers with a World-Improving Idea. This happened last century as well as now. Currently there are thousands of them. Young entrepreneurs as well as seasoned men and women, who wanted to do something else with their life and give it meaning. The source of their ideas is manifold – from a romantic idea of biological farming to a smart tech idea of a tidal energy generator. I was lucky to meet many of them and hear their inspiring stories straight from the 'horse's mouth'. I dived into many websites, blogs, books and articles to make a subjective and hopefully inspiring selection for you.

Being a member of Social Venture Network both in the USA and in Europe (The Netherlands) gave me the introduction to many inspiring businesses and the people behind these.

Tom Szaky of TerraCycle

When he was 19 years old and in his first year at Princeton University, Tom Szaky took several of his friends up to Montreal for the Fall Break of 2001. There he stayed with friends who were feeding table scraps to red wiggler worms in a composting bin and using the resultant fertilizer to feed some of their indoor plants. The results were amazing! Tom was looking for a business idea to enter into the upcoming Princeton Business Plan Contest, early the following year. He had his answer: use worms to eat organic waste. He could make a quality fertilizer and address a major environmental issue at the same time!

This idea was the start of a journey. Tom was fascinated by the process of turning waste into something valuable. The worm poop fertilizer idea grew with many ups and downs into a business. Winning awards and becoming an example of young innovators with a sustainable business. Over the years the business of TerraCyle changed. It went from worm poop fertilizer to recycling and up-cycling all kinds of packaging or waste materials that nobody else was recycling. And the good thing is that the public is included in the process. TerraCycle recycles and up-cycles waste packaging and used products that are normally difficult to recycle. Interested consumers can sign up for free on their website to collect a variety of materials and for each piece of packaging waste or used product they collect, TerraCycle contributes 2 cents to a school or charity of their choice! TerraCycle collects over 60 types of waste globally, including Capri Sun drink pouches, Frito Lay chip bags and Mars candy wrappers in the US and BIC writing instruments in The Netherlands. The collected material is up-cycled into backpacks, tote bags, park benches, bike racks and flowerpots.

TerraCycle's services keeps unnecessary trash out of the landfill (still a common practice in the USA) or incineration ovens – cutting down on carbon emissions, landfill space, and waste. TerraCycle also focuses on providing up-cycled and recycled products to consumers, so they can choose to buy items that were produced using less energy and less waste and are therefore more sustainable. In addition, TerraCycle pays to carbon offset all the shipping of waste to regional collection depots. Formed in 2002, TerraCycle developed from a simple idea with a mission into an innovative waste recycling company that does so much more than the traditional players. The development of the company shows the entrepreneurial power and the passion of its founder and the team on board. TerraCycle is a culture club: they have furnished their offices with waste materials and they hold frequent graffiti jams where their office buildings get painted. And you can imagine there is a creative non-conformist drive in the company.

Here is what Tom Szaky says on entrepreneurship: 'Entrepreneurship means the pursuit of new ideas, creation of new systems and business models in order to make a profit, but also, especially in the case of TerraCycle, to solve the world's most pressing social issues. TerraCycle's business model has changed a few times over the years, but our mission and our practice remain the same. We've moved from organic fertilizer to sponsored waste stream collection for consumer packaging and products. We've expanded from consumer programs to include business programs. We've adapted to what's best for our idea: keeping waste out of landfill and making products completely from waste so they're ultimately as sustainable as possible. Entrepreneurism is always adapting, growing and innovative.'

Loek Beeren and Frits Pannekoek of The Colour Kitchen

In Amsterdam you can go and eat in a restaurant with a mission: The Colour Kitchen. Its mission is very clear: Celebrating Diversity! The idea for the restaurant has its origin in the social unrest in some big cities in The Netherlands at the end of last century, where migrants from Northern Africa and Turkey were not integrated into Dutch society. It caused frustration with the second and third generations of the migrants and it led to crime and violence. It was the bankruptcy of the so-called 'multi cultural society'.

The Dutch government had neglected this development for a decade or three and in 2001 had the ridiculous idea to solve the problem with a communication campaign. One of the agencies that pitched for the campaign came up with a sharp analysis: the only way to steer the development in a positive direction is to include all cultures in successful work environments. An environment where people connect, where people are educated and where they become part of, and contribute to, their society. The overall business objective was to put diversity at the core of companies. One of the ideas was a restaurant where dishes of all cultures were prepared and served by people of all cultures. Bringing their culture into work and learning a trade.

The selection board at the Ministry of Home Affairs turned down the unorthodox campaign proposal, because it didn't meet the formal requests. Despite the setback, the creative team who presented saw it as an encouragement and started working on new ways to demonstrate the power of their proposal. In the years following, the tension between cultural groups in The Netherlands grew, leading to riots and murders in this, until then, innocent country by the sea.

It took 5 years to finally open the restaurant. Co-founder Loek Beeren who switched from a successful career in international hotel and restaurant chains, was the one who wholeheartedly adopted the creative idea. After helping to start up the Amsterdam branch of TV-chef Jamie Oliver's Fifteen, he opened a great restaurant in one of Amsterdam's 'problem quarters'. Situated in an old renovated school building, with over 150 seats, meeting rooms and a staff of 40 (professionals and students). Professional restaurant formula developer Frits Pannekoek joined him and gave great encouragement by involving suppliers of kitchen equipment, technical installations and food and beverages. The City's mayor also helped by securing the right permits and the Housing Corporation that owned the building gave its support with a substantial rent relief.

The restaurant was welcomed by the local community. Well, not exactly welcomed: in the first year there was a serious burglary and even an armed robbery. After 5 years and with more than 150 students going through the restaurant, a second restaurant was opened in Utrecht by Princess Maxima, and a Colour Kitchen at Work company catering branch was set up. From all over Europe entrepreneurs are now applying for a franchise of The Colour Kitchen. And yes, the company has even started to make some money and Loek now gets a salary out of it. He and Frits are real WIE's.

Gary Hirschberg of Stonyfield Farm Yogurt

Gary Hirschberg was the 'CE-Yo' of the amazing yogurt company Stonyfield, although now he has become Chairman. You must certainly read more from him in his book Stirring It Up: How to Make Money and Save the World. I like the way Stonyfield's meaningful positioning was described, introducing Gary as a key-note speaker in the 2012 conference program of Social Venture Network Europe: 'The history of commerce has always been about taking – taking from the earth, from workers, farmers and those yet to come. But at Stonyfield we have proven over nearly three decades that it doesn't have to be that way, and that actually all stakeholders can win. We call this 'win-win-win-win-win' business. Today our nearly $400 million company builds topsoils, supports hundreds of thousands of acres of chemical-free agriculture, and promotes healthier people and healthier animals. Our farmers are profitable, our employees are well-paid and supported with sabbaticals and preventative health care and our shareholders make excellent returns. This is how we invent a sustainable future.'

Stonyfield, is an organic yogurt maker located in Londonderry, New Hampshire, USA. Stonyfield Farm was founded by Samuel Kaymen in 1983, in Wilton, New Hampshire, as an organic farming school. Gary Hirschberg joined him in 1982 on his board of directors. The company makes the number-one selling brand of organic yogurt and number-three overall yogurt brand in the United States, according to Fortune magazine. In 2001, Groupe Danone, a France-based food product company, purchased an initial 40% of Stonyfield shares. This was followed in late 2003 with an additional purchase so that Group Danone now owns about 85% of Stonyfield shares. But the passion and the mission are still central. Through its Profits for the Planet program, Stonyfield  gives 10% of profits to environmental causes. Stonyfield also uses the yogurt lids –millions each week– to promote causes, organizations and environmental initiatives. The plant engineers have worked hard to reduce the energy used to make yogurt, and to recycle as much waste as possible, which has kept tens of millions of pounds of waste from being dumped into landfills. The company is proud because it is able to keep hundreds of organic farmers in business and over 100,000 acres managed with organic practices.

Adam Lowry and Eric Ryan of Method USA

The website of Method USA is one of the best I have ever seen. Most informative and fun to read. And yes the passion for clean & green is splashed in your face. There are two guys behind this revolutionary brand in soaps and household detergents, which started in 2000 with an idea. Adam Lowry and Eric Ryan, are the proud brainparents of Method and the very first people against dirty®. When I visited their offices in downtown San Francisco in July 2010 it was like walking into a very sophisticated perfume house. I had no idea that this was a company that made cleaning products and detergents. What was the idea and where did it come from?

Back in 2000, Eric was wondering why cleaning products are so poorly designed and Adam was dreaming of green cleaners that actually work and aren't stinky. Together, these two childhood friends came up with an idea to revolutionize the cleaning world with stylish, eco-friendly products made with non-toxic ingredients that clean like hell and smell like heaven. This household idea was the start of one of the fastest-growing private companies in America and one that is single-handedly turning the consumer-packaged goods industry on its head. The big players who first laughed at these new kids on the block now carefully follow the moves of Method.

Innovations from Method, such as the first triple-concentrated (3x) laundry detergent that was introduced in the US mass market in 2004 have set new industry standards. The idea drove a powerful new formula of marketing and chemical technology. Eric knew many people wanted cleaning products they didn't have to hide under their sinks and Adam knew how to make them without any dirty ingredients. Their powers combined, they set out to save the world and create an entire line of home care products that were powerful, green and packaged so sympathetically that they became true lifestyle-products.

What is their mission? 'We're in business to change business. At Method, we see our work as an amazing opportunity to redesign how cleaning products are made and used and how businesses can integrate sustainability. Our challenge is to make sure that every product we send out into the world is a little agent of environmental change, using safe and sustainable materials and manufactured responsibly. Little green soldiers in the battle of doing-well-by-doing-good, if you will. This is why we make our bottles from 100% recycled plastic, why we constantly seek to reduce the carbon emitted by our business (and why we offset the remainder), why we never test on animals, why we design innovative products using natural, renewable ingredients, and why we're transparent about the ingredients we use, how we make our products and what our track record is as a green business.'

During the visit at method I was especially interested in the culture and the do's and don'ts. Meeting Andrea Freedman, CFO of Method or 'chief financial person against dirty' was an exhilarating journey along the 'seven obsessions' of Method. These seven pillars of Method's success are inspiring for anyone who wants to set up a sustainable company:

1. Create a Culture Club. Use culture as a competitive advantage by branding from the inside out.
2. Inspire Advocates. Create advocates behind a social mission rather than just transactional customers.
3. Be a Green Giant. Personalize the green movement to inspire change on a grand scale.
4. Kick Ass Fast. If you're not the biggest, you'd better be the fastest.
5. Relationship Retail. Deliver retail differentiation by creating fewer but deeper relationships.
6. Win on Product Experience. Be product-centric and deliver remarkable product experiences.
7. Driven by Design. Build design leadership into your DNA.

All of the lessons in building up Method are told by the founders in their book 'The Method method'. I can especially recommend the 'Error Autopsy' segments where the authors dissect and explain their less successful moments in business.

Mike Hannigan, Give Something Back

'We are a totally different kind of office supply company'

Every year, Mike Hannigan, (co-founder of the Give Something Back office-supply company, in Oakland, California) and his employees calculate how much of the store's previous year's profits they can afford to give to charity. So far, the company has donated about $5 million.

Through a balloting process, the company's customers choose which charities will get 40 percent of the business' donations, employees decide on 30 percent, and Mr. Hannigan and Sean Marx, his business partner and co-founder, decide on the other 30 percent.

Speaking about branding: Give Something Back is what it says it is. Deb Nelson, the inspiring director of Social Venture Network USA introduced us to Mike Hannigan. On a technology business trip to Silicon Valley, Leen and I could drive over to Oakland and visit Mike. Just a normal office building with a lot of sales and marketing people and Mike sitting in a small corner office. His story struck us. He had this moment in life where he and his business partner started to contribute actively to society. Being a very successful sales rep in copiers, he thought about the ideals he once had in the early seventies and decided literally to give something back. I have copied some of their website texts here and I believe they are self explanatory and inspiring!

'Give Something Back is here to make the experience of buying office supplies for your business a whole lot more fun and personal while keeping prices competitive. Thanks to the company's unique giving model, profits go to hard-working nonprofit organizations who share in the Give Something Back mission to improve local communities and help the environment thrive.'

The giving model

In 1991, the founders of Give Something Back came up with a way for businesses to have a positive social impact by doing something they do anyway: buying office supplies. Seeing the huge profits the big box stores made, they thought that by being leaner, smarter and nicer they could keep prices low, develop long-term customer relationships and give millions back to their communities. They were right. Over the past 20 years, Give Something Back has donated over $5 million dollars in profits back to amazing nonprofits across the Western region of the USA. This totals 75% of the net earnings of Give Something Back.

And there is passion in the business of Give Something Back. The employees see the office supplies not as just every day stuff but as objects of radical change and the props of everyday office humor. 'We genuinely have fun doing this, and care about every aspect of what we do. When we create amazing customer experiences, you remain a happy customer, and then together we're able to keep giving back. Everyone's a winner.'

Hans van Breugel of Tocardo Tidal energy

The Dutch and water is a classic combination. They had their Golden Age in the 16th and 17th century sailing every ocean looking for trade. And since the middle ages they became specialists in keeping dry feet. Creating smart systems of dikes and dams and milling water to the sea. The newest venture is extracting energy from tidal streams. One of the world class pioneers is Hans van Breugel and his tidal turbine company Tocardo. I met Hans at one of the energy brainstorms of the province of North-Holland and was struck by his pragmatism and determination. After a career of working as a pilot on large merchant ships, Hans found new trades. He is now working in social housing developments in poor South African urban areas (with sustainable energy solutions) as well as with Tocardo. He sometimes says that he is kind of surprised himself to find a down-to-earth guy like him working on all kinds of sustainable and social ventures. If you speak to him about Tocardo you believe that tidal energy will be an important clean source of our future energy. You feel happy and grateful that guys like Hans keep pushing this technology step by step to a sustainable business. They belong to saviors of the earth.

Tocardo is a young and ambitious company from the Netherlands, aiming to become a world-wide operation and leading player in the tidal energy industry. Tocardo acts both as in-stream energy device manufacturer and tidal project developer. In 2008 a pre-commercial demonstration project based on the Tocardo Aqua T50 turbine was commissioned in one of the barrages in the Netherlands. In the same year, clean tech fund company, E2C, invested in the technology. This was the starting point of commercialization of the robust Tocardo technology that will range from 50kW to 700kW turbines. These can be placed in rivers all over the world or in sea environments with strong enough tidal currents. Placed in rivers, even in the most remote places, they can supply energy with high reliability to local communities. Preventing the burning of wood or gasoline for generators and making the building of eco-system damaging dams less needed.

Tocardo's mission is to contribute to clean, affordable and predictable energy. Tocardo is fully aware of the huge challenge our world is facing in replacing the need for fossil fuels in the coming decades. Tidal stream and river stream energy are among the key sources of renewable energy available on our planet. Tocardo is looking to harvest this energy and provide clean and sustainable energy to future generations. 'I firmly believe people want green energy but they will always end up going for the energy source that is the most reliable and the most cost effective. So keeping it simple and building up is the key.' 'The only way to start tidal power projects is with simple turbines which do not have gear mechanisms that can go wrong and need a lot of maintenance. And the beauty is that, unlike wind, you never see the turbines, they're totally submerged.'

TOCARDO BV
INTERNATIONAL

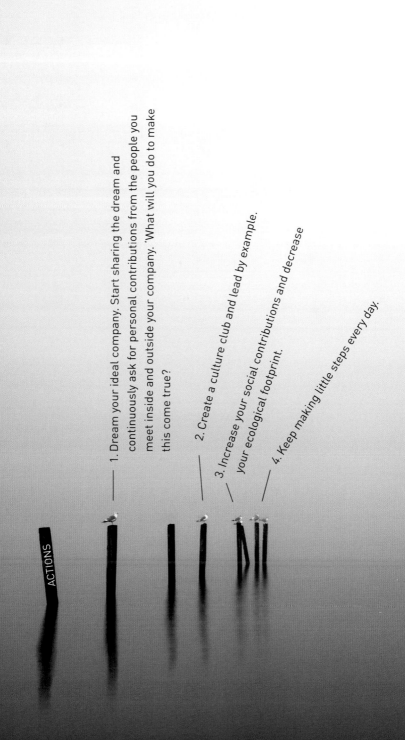

ACTIONS

1. Dream your ideal company. Start sharing the dream and continuously ask for personal contributions from the people you meet inside and outside your company. 'What will you do to make this come true?

2. Create a culture club and lead by example.

3. Increase your social contributions and decrease your ecological footprint.

4. Keep making little steps every day.

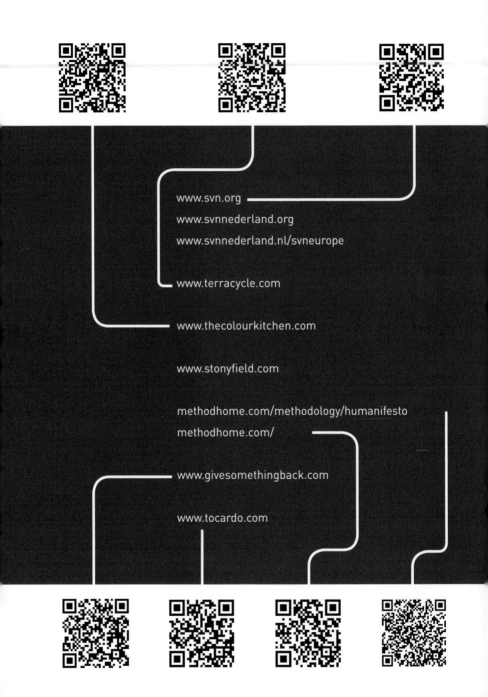

www.svn.org

www.svnnederland.org

www.svnnederland.nl/svneurope

www.terracycle.com

www.thecolourkitchen.com

www.stonyfield.com

methodhome.com/methodology/humanifesto

methodhome.com/

www.givesomethingback.com

www.tocardo.com

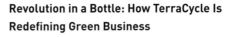

Revolution in a Bottle: How TerraCycle Is Redefining Green Business
Tom Szaky, ISBN 978-1591842507

Stirring It Up: How to Make Money and Save the World
Gary Hirshberg, IBN 978-1401303440

The Method Method
Seven Obsessions That Helped Our Scrappy Start-Up Turn an Industry Upside Down
Eric Ryan and Adam Lowry,
ISBN 978-1591843993

'If we maintain the present, we are certain to lose a better future. To seize that better future, we must go beyond what is considered best today.' (Gunter Pauli)

START DOING BEFORE THINKING

→ Start by doing, not planning
→ Keep moving your feet
→ Get protection from your leaders

Although many books have been written about the importance of doing, our academic and careful society has become much more planning oriented. So, if it is a company that you want to start, or a book you want to write, or a new political party you want to establish, every process starts with planning. Of course, I can hear you think, how else should you start? You cannot do anything without planning first.

Well, that has yet to be seen.

First of all, we always think and plan in our subconscious. Lots of planning and thinking goes on in our lives without us being fully aware of it. But the main risk we run with planning too much is the fact that it hinders us big time from acting. It becomes an exercise in futility.

We have to be realistic. Quite often we are afraid of the consequences we might face when we fail in our endeavours. And because we do not want to fail, we plan, plan and plan again. We go through all kinds of scenarios; we build optimistic, realistic and pessimistic plans; we make budgets accordingly and discuss these over and over with both internal and external advisors.

It is like discussing our plans with the fire brigade while our building is burning down.

By the way, the reason that crises are actually worthwhile and interesting is because they quite often force organizations into action. We are forced to do something. We often end up calling negative events a 'blessing in disguise'. For example: 'I always wanted to start my own company and because I was fired I had a reason to begin.' The negative fact of being fired translates itself into the positive fact of starting your own company. These blessings in disguise happen time after time. But then again, let's not wait for this blessing in disguise. Let's not wait to become a sustainable company before it is too late. Let's start now.

Since I have been lecturing about sustainability and long-term approaches to building companies (as described in my book 'Rip Off Your Necktie and Dance') I have had many discussions with people about building strategies and companies and found that simple things that are close to us are often overlooked and forgotten.

The most simple and elementary law is that it is easier to turn the wheels of a car when you are driving than when that car is standing still. Certainly when there was no power steering it was almost impossible to turn the wheels when standing still. Imagine that your company (or even yourself) is a car. When you want to move around freely and do what you want, you have to start moving first. A boxer that is standing still will lose a fight almost immediately. Boxers have to move around like dancers (float like butterflies, sting like bees). That's why boxing takes so much energy, I can tell you this from experience.

So, what do we learn from this law? We learn that we have to start moving before we can start to change direction. We have to start before we think!

It is our wish and ambition to build a sustainable company. Step number one is to start doing anything, it doesn't matter what. And that process of starting to move is so very unnatural that hardly any program will begin like that.

Cut the corporate crap

'First we have to form a steering committee, with people in it that know what they are talking about and that steering committee should meet at least twice per month to discuss plans. After they have built their solid plans with solid budgets, they have to present them to the Board who meet and talk about it on several occasions. Do not forget to look at best practices in other companies, so we do not make the same mistakes. And oh yeah, by the way, do not forget the different reporting mechanisms that exist and out of which we have to select one. Talk to other companies about their experiences with these reporting mechanisms. Budget is important and various scenarios should be taken into account.'

Everybody knows this kind of language. Sounds reasonable huh? But it is THE way to kill any initiative. It is THE way to take the Passion away. And without Passion... no sustainable sustainability.

The way to take passion out of a process is by discussing it to death, over and over again. The way to bring passion into any process is by starting to move. Things are beginning to happen, people are seeing what you do and start to believe. Wow, what is going on there, I want to be part of that!

Well, I guess I have made my point now. Starting a process to build a sustainable company, be it a new company or transforming an existing company, is to BEGIN DOING THINGS. Be a human doing not a human being!

In our own company we defined a goal, 5 years away. In hindsight, thinking about the long-term goals at Mars, these 5 years were not long-term at all. But anyway, who cares how long-term this goal is. Say anything, set any goal, it really doesn't matter very much what goals you set, it matters how quickly you start moving.

We however, defined that we wanted to have a 100% sustainable company by the end of 2014. That was it, nothing more, nothing less. Nobody new what that goal meant, we had not made any plans, we had not made definitions of what sustainability really means. We just started by defining a goal and went with it.

We started by defining projects, which we thought would help us on our way and of which we thought to be sustainable. We never discussed the sustainability elements too much but went to work. We asked our employees to decide on which 10 projects they would want to spend their private time and went to work. No budgets, no plans, no hard goals, just beginning. What great fun it was and what passion did it create. And the good thing about these kind of more or less undefined projects is that anything is possible. Everybody helps, in every place in the organization. People are all equal (are all Associates in Mars' terms) and work on the projects together. You can even say, in old-fashioned organizational thinking, all of the projects started bottom-up.

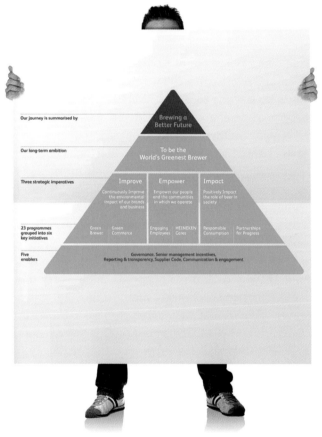

Improve, Empower, Impact. Check out www.heinekeninternational.com and find out how engaging employees take the central position in their sustainable strategy.

And when projects start bottom-up, or start throughout all layers of the organization if you wish, there is no need to stimulate people to work on it. The projects are theirs, the success is theirs and the energy is their passion. This also applies of course to the people you need in order to become a sustainable company: the entrepreneurs – the self starting, decisive, innovative, daring people. Some others will sulk and choose the side-lines and leave with or without encouragement. That's the natural selection process you shouldn't be afraid of, it will solve the disadvantage of not having started from scratch.

It really is easy, BUT it can only work when top management is behind it, because at certain points decisions have to be taken. For example, if you would define sustainability with the three P's (and yes, forgetting the fourth P again) you can define projects on the basis of that. And since people translate sustainability often with the word 'green', the quick step is to define a car policy based upon carbon dioxide emissions. Defining a car policy project seems to be the first step every time. Well fine, go with it. Who cares what you do, as long as you are moving!

Problems guaranteed!

Soon after starting the project on CO_2 emissions you run into all kinds of problems anyway. Problems like; how high do we set our targets; what do other companies do; what is realistic; what kind of cars do we currently drive; do we have a baseline, a basis upon which we want to measure our future improvements? Do we link this car policy to a larger vision on mobility? How do we make a link with public transportation? What is our policy on travel anyway? How do we use modern technologies like Skype and Microsoft Lync to be able to communicate electronically? Are there differences between countries? etc.

It is easy to see that even when we have made a start to get moving, the machine immediately grinds to a halt. And here we are again. After making the bold decision to move and do before we think, the machine immediately stops after the first small move. There we are again; no power steering and a car standing still. What's next?

The trick is to keep moving at all times! When I was young and in high-school in Texas, I played American football. What I learned there was that throughout the game your feet had to stay in motion. When people wanted to tackle you; when you had not decided yet what direction to move; your feet had to be moving constantly. Even when staying in the same place, keep your feet going boy!

So, we have decided to start with sustainability. We are first moving before thinking, we have defined some internal projects and we have given people freedom to go. Every question that comes up, decide immediately and keep going. Don't worry about wrong decisions, because you can improve on them at any time later. Just keep moving. What should the emission maximum of CO_2 on cars be? Doesn't matter, just set one. What should we do regarding public transportation? Nothing yet, keep it simple. What should we do with modern technologies to communicate and diminish our need to travel anyway? Use Skype, because it is available, free and easy to use. Move on, move on, move on. Keep it simple, take decisions and do not waste too much time on meetings. Be pragmatic, keep budgets low or even at zero, and try to show to your company that you are making money.

The many sceptical people around you will think about the cost of these sustainability programs and will use that against you. You can help yourself by earning money for the company; that usually shuts them up and makes them think (DO).

The people who started our program helped themselves tremendously by calculating vigorously how much money they were making for the company. How they were (and they were indeed) making their salaries back. Making immediate savings by installing LED lighting; immediate savings by using less gasoline that the company had to buy and so on and so on and so on.

They even defined a social game by publishing a list every month showing which people used the least gas per kilometre. Of course, people always want to be number one, or at least high on the list. No one planned this, they just got on and did it and it was a great idea.

Do not let the company policy and bureaucracy take over the project. Because any company has the tendency to try to take control of any project that goes on within its borders. So, as soon as people have identified a project that goes on within their territory people will want to get involved to protect themselves against it.

Beware of the bureaucrats! Protection is needed from the highest level within the organization to survive.

Give your GO!

What we have seen on many occasions is that indeed high-level support is essential for sustainability projects to survive. Particularly when you go for the entrepreneurial approach as described above. The passion has to sink in steadily, but slowly and surely the projects will become the driving elements of the so-called standing organization.

High-level support is necessary specially when you want to force people to move or use results. For example, it is necessary that top management gives their GO to a new car policy. Otherwise the company will not go for it. There are reasons enough not to do anything on sustainability. In our organization, our managers in Spain initially thought that employees there would not be interested in sustainability. Well, this was wrong thinking because at least 30% of all employees wanted to be involved. And because all of our German managers drove an A8, the car policy was unimplementable in that country. When managers themselves keep driving high polluting cars, there is not authenticity. I gave a lecture for a group of 400 top managers about sustainability at a sustainability conference. My first question to the audience was 'Who thinks sustainability is important?' Of course everyone raised their hands, it was after all a sustainability conference. Why else would they be there!

Second question was 'Who in this audience is a leader?' Most hands were raised again. My final question was 'How is it then possible that you as leaders, having to set an example on sustainability, all drive in these big polluting cars that I see in the parking lot? What about your credibility? Don't you care yourself and don't you want your employees to care? What about authenticity?

Well, as you can imagine, the audience was 'not amused' by my remarks and criticism. But this point exactly shows one of the major shortcomings in a sustainability program or initiative. When leadership fails or is just not visible, the program dies a quick death. Leaders have to set active examples; practice what you preach is a saying that is extremely true but apparently difficult to perform. Leaders can also be an unnecessary anchor in programs by constantly asking for justifications, proof, documents, plans and scenarios.

Leaders can also set an example by giving freedom of action to their people. Trusting them to set the goals and do things.

Well then, are we going to set plans or don't we? Yes, of course we make plans, of course we write documents. In my opinion we do everything that always is being done, but in a different order. After a year of working in a more or less uncoordinated fashion it is about time to harvest. At that point in time we have to see were we stand and where we have to adjust. We adjust, redefine our goals if necessary, report on how far we have come and then again we move forward.

So, after a period of about one year, once we have built up some of the momentum we need to keep us moving, we have the time to see what has happened. We can measure and compare with others; we can take a quick look at benchmarks; we can publish what we have accomplished. We can and should be proud on what we have done. Communication about this is of the utmost importance and often heavily under-estimated. I would say that maybe 50% of success of these kinds of projects and their long-term survival depends on well defined communications. Share the results over and over again. Open up discussions on all levels of your company. Ask for everybody's opinions and ideas and use them.

But one thing: KEEP MOVING!

Tips for starting your sustainability initiatives

1. **Do not set a budget** for becoming sustainable; make money with it (helps keep the critics away).

2. **Start with projects** in your direct sphere of influence, so you don't need permission.

3. **Contact people** who think like you, there are many great clubs and communities of social ventures. Every country has more than one.

4. **Find one or more sponsors** in higher management levels, or even outside of the company (might even help to convince your own management!

5. **Look for business opportunities**; customers or suppliers who would like to cooperate with you in your projects, even might help finance them.

6. **Open blogs**, yammer, twitter and other community communications, so the word spreads both inside and outside of your company.

'In a world where populations are growing, where natural resources are stressed, where communities are forced to do more with less and where consumers' expectations are expanding, sustainability is core to our business continuity and survival.' (Muhtar Kent, CEO Coca Cola)

MAKE BUSINESS, IT'S GOOD FOR YOUR CUSTOMERS

→ Making money by being sustainable
→ What do your customers feel?
→ Customers want to be with you
→ Use customers to become sustainable

We are doing business, we are running a company or we want to start up a company. And we want to be sustainable. Why is it that many companies seem to be having problems in becoming sustainable? The answer is very simple or we should at least make it simple. Sustainability is not very high on the priority list of many managers because they have other issues to worry about. Or at least, they think they have other issues to worry about.

Normal day-to-day management has to do with questions like 'how do we survive this crisis', 'what is the budget for next year, next month or next quarter and how can we make that', 'how can we make our shareholders happy', and many other questions like that.

And yes, if you read this well you will say we are missing something, there is nothing about customers in this list. And to be bloody honest with you, customers are not high on the priority list in any company. This fact will be denied by everybody you ask, but sorry, it's true. Customers are normally not high on any managers' lists. Why is that then? Well, that is not so easy to answer and I have been struggling with that question during my whole career, constantly pushing people back into the market, towards customers.

It is sad to see that in many instances people and ideas do not start with customers, because it would make the world so much easier. When one starts a company, one starts with making a business-plan. Wouldn't it be much easier to start talking to customers or potential customers first? Do a real market analysis, by physically moving into the real world and meet with people. No market research bureaus or internet investigations. No, open the door and go outside to physically meet people! Dangerous and sometimes embarrassing, but always worthwhile. A budget for next year should also be based upon the opinion of customers, which is hardly ever the case. Because the opinion of your customers should steer everything you do. Constructing a sustainable company should be based upon the opinion of your existing or potentially new customers.

In our company we have started several new and innovative ideas. The ideas we started by immediately exposing customers to our thoughts and visiting them to talk about our not yet fully developed plans were much more successful than the innovations that were internally developed, put in plans and brochures and finally, at the very end, were presented to our customers.

My advice is to start with customers immediately in anything that you do. Anything? Yes, anything. If it's not exactly clear what you are going to do, share your doubts and incompleteness with your customer. This in itself will be highly rewarded.

Share your sustainable thoughts with your customers.

So, when you want to become a sustainable company, share that thought with your customer immediately. We did that with one of our largest customers, who of course immediately asked me what we meant by that thought. We shared a couple of hours of brainstorming, during which it was completely clear to my customer that we did not know exactly how to move forward. He didn't know it either and they had the same ambitions on sustainability, like many companies have. The coincidence was (and coincidence does not exist of course) that this customer was working on his own long-term sustainable strategy and was looking for a partner, which we of course gladly would like to be.

At the end of the meeting we came to that partnership issue. He asked me if we wanted to be their partner for the future and I said yes, like many of my competitors had done as well. The customer answered 'we would very much like for you to be our partner, because you are the only company that has openly shared their thoughts, doubts and failures with us. All of your competitors seem to know it all, which can never be true. And since we are also on a path towards the future, let's walk it together.'

Sharing thoughts, ideas and ambitions with customers is rarely done, but immensely rewarding.

Let your customers drive your business

So, coming back to the beginning. The question 'Why become sustainable?' could be posed to your customers. Suppose that your customers like it and want to belong to you when you select that strategy, would there be any doubt in your mind? When your customers drive your future, is that so bad? Of course not, it should be the dream scenario of any company. But in order for your customers to do so, you need to be speaking on the same level with each other and be in an equal position to discuss the topic. And in many companies, such relationships with customers do not exist at all. And that is caused by the fact that most companies never speak with their customers. They either sell consumer products in as large a quantity as possible, or they have a so-called business-to-business relationship, also selling products. But in both cases, no real relationship exists.

Continuous dialog with all stakeholder groups helps BMW to identify trends early, strengthen its commitment to society and reach its sustainability goals. Read about it at www.bwmgroup.com

By relationship I mean that you can feel something when doing business, it's not just any company you are doing business with. When I buy a Mars-bar, I have a feeling about the brand. When I fill up my car with Shell gasoline, I have a feeling for the brand, which goes beyond the product. I'm not just buying a candy bar or gasoline. I'm buying Mars and Shell. When one does business with Qurius (my company) people have feelings as well, good or bad. Preferably my customers feel good when hearing my company's name, of course. We're working on that – we want our customers to feel very good whenever they're in contact with Qurius. With Qurius we're making this transition, from just a supplier to a welcome and valued brand. Not with costly, over-promising impersonal advertising campaigns. We're doing this by building sustainable relations with our customers and becoming a sustainable company – adding value and being meaningful by offering solutions that help them to sustain and to become sustainable.

The market in general is changing, we all know that. Consumers themselves are becoming more and more sustainable and healthy, there is no way out of that development. Knowing that this is what customers want more and more in the future, it is where you should be heading when you are in consumer products. Tell your customers that. But realize one important thing; customers do not want to be lied to, neither now nor ever. That simple fact has never changed, it has even become stronger. And the effects caused when lying have become more horrendous than they were in the past, because of social media – and luckily so. With Twitter, Facebook and other social networks, any lie or inconsistency in your behavior is shared worldwide in a split second. Lying kills your brand. And will kill your company.

What then to do when you want to become sustainable but do not know how? Ask your customers. Tell them about your intentions and your worries and ask what they would do. Wow, you are building a strong link with your customers here. In the B2B market that is even easier to do. Tell your customers what you are doing in the field of sustainability and that you want to do that with them! And, you need their advice. You will get it immediately, I assure you. Of course, you will only get it from them if they believe that your question to them is authentic. Again, no lying here.

My company is in the B2B market and in general such companies have a smaller number of customers. Whereas Unilever has hundreds of millions of customers, we have thousands.

Involving customers in building a sustainable company is by far the strongest weapon and it takes away any doubts with other stakeholders. If your customers want it and are even willing to pay for it, who in their right mind would stop it. Protect yourself therefore with the empathy and involvement of your customers. Remember, it takes away all criticism from others if your customers are behind you.

All right now, we are going to involve customers. But in what and how exactly? We want to make money by becoming sustainable. Yes, that's a big change from the past. Many companies strongly believe that they can make money by becoming sustainable. Can you make money with it, is that possible? Should you make money with it? Is that decent? These questions immediately come up when one wants to make money with sustainability. Of course these questions are nonsense. If making money helps companies to become sustainable, just go for it. And as a matter of fact, it is easy to make money being sustainable.

And there are many ways of making money by being sustainable. First of all, internally one can think of many products and projects which save money, like less gasoline in cars or less electricity when using LED. But we are talking about customers here, which means that we are in the open market and that our own internal savings bring money, but do not count in this strategy. We are talking and thinking here about projects in the marketplace with our customers. What do they need? And that is exactly the big point I want you to aim at.

It is a big mistake that your customers would not be interested in your sustainability efforts. They are interested in it in the first place, because they need to be sustainable themselves in order to survive. My statement is that companies that are not sustainable five years from now will not survive. And since the top management of all of our and your customers is worrying about their own survival, sustainability is top of mind with them too.

Let me give you an example. Mercedes and all other big car brands know one thing. If their products, their cars, are not going to be sustainable very soon, they will be out of business. So, they have sent instructions to all of their sub contractors that they should get green-certified and they should prove that all of their products are sustainable. If they are not able to do so, they can no longer sell and they will be out of business... this year! Being sustainable is a matter of survival for any company for all kinds of reasons, but most of all for business reasons. Getting assignments from government institutions already requires a declaration of green behavior.

So, in order to survive every company has to be sustainable. All of your customers therefore have a strategic necessity to change themselves and they could use your help. Do you have any help to offer them then? Well, first of all you have your own struggle and that struggle helps them. You're in the same situation as any other company in the world.

Sharing thoughts can be done and we do that in so-called Business Dialogues. Our company prepares half day sessions to meet with the boards of our customers, discussing their long-term plans, ambitions and dreams. And I will probably not surprise you when I tell you that on every agenda in every meeting is the topic 'How to become sustainable.'

Here's one: Create a stronger bond with your customers by sharing visions and ambitions.

Two years ago I asked the CEO of one of the largest ICT firms what they were offering the market in the field of sustainability. His answer was that they had a very interesting car policy, bringing back the CO_2 outlet of their cars. And he bluntly told me that they did not think they could do more. I had to understand; they were only a consulting firm and not a production firm that could do all kinds of sustainable things with their production process. But now we know better; there is Green ICT 1.0, which tells us how we can improve our ICT usage from a sustainability perspective. But there is something far more interesting and that is called Green ICT 2.0, which means that we should use ICT to improve ourselves.

Every company should think about the question of which products they can make and bring to the market that will help their customers to become more sustainable. That is relatively easy for product companies, because they can easily define this, but it becomes more difficult for services companies, of which we have many in Western Europe. If you define products that you sell and deliver to your customers, and these products help them to become more sustainable, you win their support easily. Let customers drive your sustainability effort!

One of the most heard questions is 'What to do when my manager does not want to help us in our sustainability efforts?' It is a very real, disturbing nuisance, because if you remember the beginning of this chapter, the priority list of most managers does not have sustainability high on it. Definitely not when other issues, like crisis and survival are on it. How can you win their attention?

By going to customers and using their support. That means that you have to define programs and ideas that are in the interest of your customers. And again going back to the beginning of this chapter; the customers will decide themselves what they like or not. So, always start by going to them before anything else. Do not define sustainable products and finish them completely before you ask your customers' opinion. Start with their opinion.

Using the customer to win your projects and bring sustainability to a higher platform within your company is one of the strongest weapons you have. Use it, it is much easier than you think.

Tips & Tricks

1. Do you know what your customers think about sustainability? Find out by asking them personally. By going and visiting them.

2. Visit the 'low hanging fruit', the customers of whom you are certain they care about the subject.

4. Act as a beginner who needs help, the help of your customers. People are inclined to give it.

3. Find out their vision and ideas and ask them how you can help them. They know what you do, so maybe they have an idea about cooperation.

5. Try to define at least one product, made by you, that your customers could be interested in... after having talked to many of them.

6. When you have found that one (or more) product your customers are interested in, get their support and bring this proposal to your management. It might be a lot easier to convince them to go for it.

7. It will definitely happen when you co-develop it with your customers.

ALL FOR SUSTAINABILITY!

JEROEN DE HAAS

(CEO ENECO)

world
Improving
Entrepreneur

'Our strategy is in many ways hugely successful,' says Jeroen de Haas at the start of our interview. Jeroen, having been CEO of the energy company Eneco for many years, understands perfectly that his company can be excellent in operations but will never be able to differentiate itself in a very competitive commodity market like energy.

Besides the fact that his company is selling a commodity, it also had to face a large distrust from the general audience, his customers. The distrust came from the fact that the way the energy world operates is not very transparent for the market and this is translated in a general distrust against anything that goes wrong within Eneco.

Eneco has been looking for ways to solve this big 'trust-gap' between them and society in general.

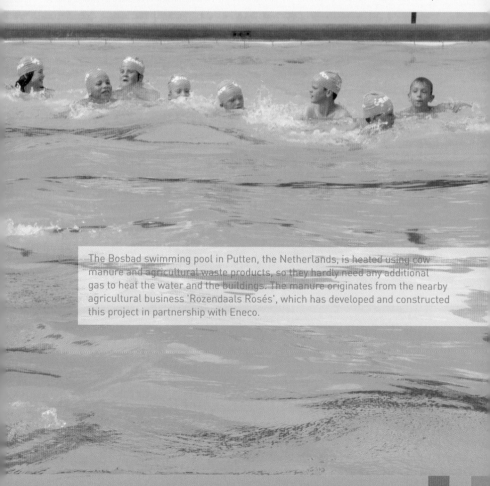

The Bosbad swimming pool in Putten, the Netherlands, is heated using cow manure and agricultural waste products, so they hardly need any additional gas to heat the water and the buildings. The manure originates from the nearby agricultural business 'Rozendaals Rosés', which has developed and constructed this project in partnership with Eneco.

So, improving the relationship between the company and its environment has been one of the most important tasks of Jeroen. And when he talks about environment he means customers, citizens, the neighborhood and the country, so it is the broadest meaning of the word. Because the environment has many faces in his opinion.

It started by him setting extremely ambitious goals, like becoming 50% sustainable in 15 years. In the baseline measurement they made at the moment of this statement, the company was 3% sustainable, so the challenge was huge. Setting this extreme goal out of his own belief was difficult to explain in the very operational company Eneco was at that time.

But wow, what a result the company achieved over time. Each year the company invests over 900 million Euros in all kinds of new technologies to produce energy, doing that in many countries. And the great thing about this is that these investments are not started by Jeroen, but his whole company is involved.

Eneco did not have the advantage of being a family owned business, like Mars and Van Gansewinkel, about whom you will read more later on in the book, but the company was and still is owned by 60 cities, which in a sense also is sustainable and long-term oriented. So that helps Eneco to get the space and time it needs to rebuild from purely operational to long-term sustainable.

And remember the customer loyalty, being a big issue in the past, has improved tremendously. But the company has to keep on giving examples and prove to the world of its intentions; like their definite choice not to produce energy with coal and nuclear plants. In order to be trusted they surround themselves with organizations like Greenpeace and WWF. Greenpeace selected Eneco to be 'the winner of tomorrow' and WWF is testing the company in many ways like their CO_2 output, their clarity and transparency in their goals. Eneco and WWF perform projects together and support each other.

Jeroen states clearly that the sustainable vision for the future was perceived as relevant by the employees, a crucial element in its success. In his opinion this perceived relevance is necessary to create stickiness for this vision within the company. Also, translating the vision to every single employee of Eneco is helping it to last. For example, what does the vision mean to every technician of Eneco in his everyday job and how can the receptionist use it on a daily basis? By being trustworthy, friendly and helpful, they can build up long-term, sustainable, relationships with their customers. And this represents an enormous economic value and advantage.

And so, slowly but surely, Eneco is transforming itself. This is clear to see for Jeroen and his teams, but still a little away from its customers and potential customers. Which does not matter very much, because it will come to them as soon as they feel and live it. And that time will come eventually, for sure.

But today Eneco looks for simple, understandable ways to communicate with its customers. Like, for example, their successful activity 'Dutch Wind'. Eneco has a huge contingent of windmills, both on the sea and land, producing electricity. This is Dutch energy, produced by Dutch wind. Easy to explain to the customers from which windmill their specific energy comes. And when the wind blows harder, the energy price goes down. The consumers are tied, one-on-one, to the energy-producing units. It feels like they own them themselves. And bringing energy to the consumers, making it explicit to them, created the success of this campaign.

But Eneco wants to go even further. The company wants to involve its customers in the production of energy. And the three key words in that vision are Sustainability, De-central and Together. Sustainable in producing 'clean' energy. De-central in moving from big-scale, far-away energy producing units towards small-scale energy producers in the neighborhoods of people. And Together in doing nothing ever any more without involving the customers.

These ambitious goals will transform Eneco from a hardware-owning, facility company into a company that connects producers and users of energy, turning producers into users and visa versa. Becoming a clear-inghouse for sustainable energy. Like Spotify is doing for music, Eneco will be doing for energy; connecting people. Wow!

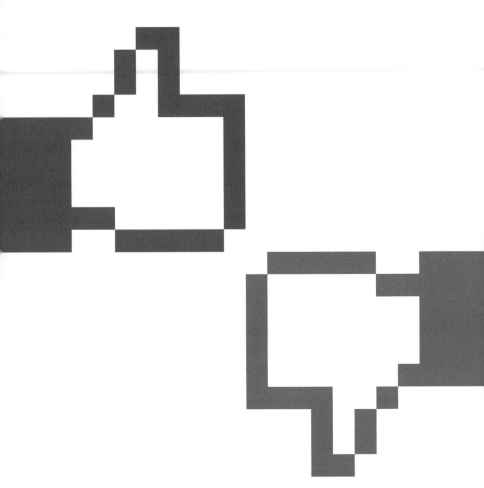

'In a world increasingly filled with deliberately and sensationally staged experiences... consumers choose to buy or not buy based on how real they perceive an offering to be.' (Pine & Gilmore)

SUSTAINABILITY REQUIRES TRANSPARENCY

→ You're being watched!

→ How to avoid greenwashing?

→ Walk the talk! (First walk, then talk)

CHAPTER 8

The era of sustainability has brought a new challenging dimension to company branding that is changing the setting of communications for good. Exaggerating and overpromising in communications hasn't appeared to disturb anyone so far. It is generally accepted as being an inherent part of the marketing game, with companies' promises in branding taken very seriously. For years 'new', 'cleaner', 'better', 'improved', – whatever superlative, it was okay. But for sustainable claims it doesn't work like this. As soon as you display yourself as being sustainable, or worse, you put yourself forward for being sustainable, every word counts, as your actions do.

As a sustainable company, you're being watched. Not only by environmentalists, but by everyone. Consumers might not jump on your sustainable offerings as soon as you market them, but they will check if you're keeping your sustainable promises. And if you don't, they're able to adjust your reputation worldwide within seconds by typing up to 140 characters.

Scary? Yes and no. We'll come to that in a second. First we'll look at the most interesting aspect of this development. The fact that your branding is taken seriously, that's something to celebrate. How come that people consider your words so closely when it comes to sustainability? Because they care. Customers do care and are touched by a sustainable message. That's to be rejoiced. And why does it touch them? Well, we're all consumers, so let's just face it, it's easy. We all know that we should care for the planet. We all know that we're running out of fossil energy sources within two generations. And we all know that we'll have to adjust our lifestyle for future generations to have an enjoyable life and a live-able planet too. We are still polluting like there's no life after ours, as if we have no children.

We all know, but do we want to know?

Anyone looking at this is putting their finger on the 'weak' spot. Since governments are slow movers in the field of sustainability, companies take the lead as they have to. Companies are the messengers – putting their fingers where it hurts, talking about responsibilities, the planet... Yes, that's suspicious, since it's a change. It is hardly surprising that consumers feel a distrust towards companies that all of a sudden have 'good' intentions. For years and years most companies didn't seem to care, and here they are, telling everyone that they care, and that I as a consumer should care too.

Everywhere in my book I'm encouraging you not to hesitate for a second. I keep on telling you, just start being sustainable, there is no time to lose. But at this point I'm advising you to think twice. Not too long of course, you should know me by now, but be aware. Once you've decided to really become a sustainable company, and you start to share this through communications, there's no way back. People will be watching you. This is not about selling chocolate and promising that people will feel better eating your chocolate brand. Or guaranteeing that the deodorant your customer buys will attract dozens of people from the opposite sex. Once you enter the world of sustainability, you're talking real – responsibilities, caring, action, generations, climate, world.

Back to the reasons why every word counts when it comes to sustainability. Customers do care, that's one reason. The other reason is that other companies have messed up in recent years, by promising much, talking about the world, big words about the climate and meanwhile... see what has happened! There's even an 'official' word for it, green-washing. Greenpeace helps consumers to make the difference by defining 4 green-wash criteria. Criteria worth considering before branding yourself as being a sustainable company. You're just following rules and regulations and nothing more, but meanwhile in communications you declare yourself a

PUMAVision

JANUARY, 2010

At PUMA, we believe that our position as the creative leader in Sportlifestyle gives us the opportunity and the responsibility to contribute to a better world for the generations to come. A better world in our vision—PUMAVision—would be safer, more peaceful, and more creative than the world we know today. The 4Keys is the tool we have developed to help us stay true to PUMAVision, and we use it by constantly asking ourselves if we are being Fair, Honest, Positive, and Creative in everything we do. We believe that by staying true to our values, inspiring the passion and talent of our people, working in sustainable, innovative ways, and doing our best to be Fair, Honest, Positive, and Creative, we will keep on making the products our customers love, and at the same time bring that vision of a better world a little closer every day.

Through the programs of puma.safe (focusing on environmental and social issues), puma.peace (supporting global peace) and puma.creative (supporting artists and creative organizations), we are providing real and practical expressions of this vision and building for ourselves and our stakeholders, among other things, a more sustainable future.

Posted in: Vision
Tags: Mission
Permalink: PUMAVision

ShareThis

PUMA sets a great example by putting all those sustainable marketing C's and P's into 4 relevant pillars: fair, honest, positive and creative. By doing so, it offers a clear framework to all employees and every stakeholder understands what they can count on. Get inspired by reading the PUMA vision on www.puma.com.

world-saver? That's one. You're putting more budget into sustainable branding than in actual sustainable projects? Here's two. Your CEO gives lectures about corporate social responsibility whilst your lobbyist works behind the scenes on less sustainable topics? And finally number four, you're simply branding yourself as green and responsible, whilst your products or activities are inherently polluting or unsustainable – yeah, that's a green-washer by any definition.

Walk the talk. That's the minimum. Not only for Greenpeace. But also for your customers. Do like BMW. They withdrew from Formula One in 2009 and re-directed the budget to the development of new drive technologies and sustainable projects. Easy? No. 'Of course, this was a difficult decision for us,' explained Dr. Norbert Reithofer, the chairman of the BMW board. 'But it's a resolute step in view of our company's strategic realignment. Premium will increasingly be defined in terms of sustainability and environmental compatibility. This is an area in which we want to remain in the lead. Our Formula One campaign is thus less a key promoter for us.' That's putting the money where the mouth is. That's becoming sustainable.

As a sustainable company doing the right things, there's nothing scary about the alertness of customers and NGO's. They can even become your most credible ambassadors, like Eneco experienced. In 2008 and 2009 Greenpeace declared this sustainable energy company to be the 'cleanest energy producer in The Netherlands'. And in 2011 they stimulated clients of Eneco's largest competitors in the Dutch market, Nuon and Essent, to switch to Eneco and two other sustainable energy suppliers, since both Nuon and Essent were planning to build another coal plant (whilst claiming to be sustainable in their campaigns). With over 60,000 people reacting to this very visible campaign, Nuon agreed to freeze their plans for 5 years (whereas Greenpeace's battle with Essent still continues).

Concerning sustainable branding, there's a whole lot of information that can help you out, like you'll find on sustainable-marketing. com. Not 3 or 4 Ps, but many Cs like Core, Co-operative, Credible, Consumer Benefits, Conversational, Consistency, Commitment, and Continuity. At our company Qurius we try to keep it simple by saying 'we care and we go for it', but these Cs are definitely in our approach. As a ninth one I would like to add – Clear.

Clear
Pronunciation: /klɪə/

1. easy to perceive, understand, or
   interpret (leaving no doubt; obvious
   or unambiguous; having or feeling
   no doubt or confusion)
2. transparent; unclouded (free of
   cloud, mist, or rain; pure and
   intense)
3. free of any obstructions or unwanted
   objects (free of anything that impairs
   logical thought; free of guilt)
(Oxford Dictionaries)

Books

Greenwash: The Reality Behind Corporate Environmentalism,
Jed Greer and Kenny Bruno, ISBN 978-0945257776

The Green Marketing Manifesto,
John Grant, ISBN 978-0470723241

Greener Products: The Making and Marketing of Sustainable Brands,
Al Iannuzzi, ISBN 978-1439854310

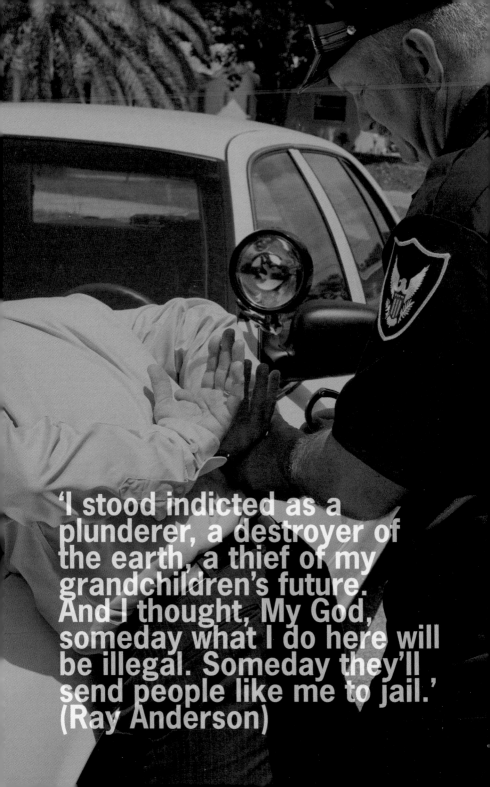

'I stood indicted as a plunderer, a destroyer of the earth, a thief of my grandchildren's future. And I thought, My God, someday what I do here will be illegal. Someday they'll send people like me to jail.' (Ray Anderson)

NEW LEADERSHIP IS DARING

→ Leaders will be sued for neglect
→ It has to strike you like lightning
→ Be consistent, persistent and find followers

Some time ago I was giving a speech to a group of about 100 CEOs. The topic was sustainability and the organizing company had asked me to make it into a shocking experience. How to do that without insulting these people and keep them listening. I decided to present a daring statement to them, something many of them are afraid of. When people are afraid, they worry. When people are in a state of shock, they might move. And what I wanted is to make these CEOs move. Or let me be more humble; what I wanted is to make at least one CEO move.

Because let's be very clear and specific, nothing is going wrong in such a terrible way that the majority of our leadership sees a need to change. Well, maybe some see a need to change, but the trouble it takes to change is far too big. People like change, but people do not like TO change. So, we all have to realize that leadership in general has other things to worry about, or so they think. So, change is not about to happen. Things need to be far worse than they are today. Unfortunately so, because of course, many people tell us that when things have become much worse, change might be useless.

Back to the speech. I decided to accuse them of terrible wrong-doings and paint a picture in which they all would go to jail. Now, that might sound like an unbelievable story to tell to people, but within the changing world of lawsuits being prevalent and people being charged with something long after they have left organizations, it is not so difficult to do.

Suppose in today's newspaper you saw the picture of one of the leaders of a large multinational being accused of a crime against nature. What a horrible thought that must be to people, because with the current state of the media, the stigma that such an image creates will never completely fade away. Again, in a nationwide newspaper we see one complete page filled with the picture of a famous CEO and a clear accusation written underneath his picture. The text should  be something like 'this person knew for a long time that the production process of his company was polluting the environment and although he knew he did not do anything about it.' Like smoking cigarettes while knowing that it kills you.

So I told my group of CEOs that they all know about sustainability. They are all aware of the state of the world. They all know what their company can do about it. Still, most of them do not act. So they are liable and they will be sued for this behavior many years from now when sustainable behavior has become normal, which it eventually will.

It's the discussion about slavery; it's the discussion about colonialism; it's the discussion about producing cigarettes; it's the discussion about electric cars etc. When slavery was 'acceptable', which it never was in the eyes of normal human beings of course, selling people was not punishable. People did not go to jail for it. If you do the same thing nowadays, and slavery still happens as we all know, you go to jail when caught.

So why would you not go to jail when you do not display sustainable behavior as a leader? And though you may not be punished now, you definitely will in the future, ex post facto.

Leaders in these times do not like the thought of going to jail; do not like to be put on the spot because of an accused advertisement; do not want to take the risk of being sued many years after they have left their companies. But every leader knows the facts, they read books and we can tell them. So, willingly not making a move and not acting in a responsible way is wrong; it is neglect.

Well, I must admit, my speech created some small waves, but not nearly the tsunami it should have. People did not take me seriously.

They did not believe such a thing could ever happen. I also do not think such a thing will happen; I am certain of it!

When change is needed, pain is necessary. Just recently I read an article about a woman who started her own company. Although she always wanted to do that, she never had the guts to change. She was, in her former job, 'sitting in a nice warm comfortable bath' as she described it herself. And I can understand that very well. You want to change, but why move from this safe and comfortable zone into something uncertain? She only made the move to start for herself after she was fired. For her, being fired was a blessing in disguise. It was a great gift.

With sustainability and moving towards a better world, or at least moving to a world that lasts longer, we need the same kind of pain in my opinion. Maybe unfortunately so, but we know that the world in and of itself will continue. The planet will still be here many hundreds of millions of years from now. But if man is still in charge, it is not certain at all. The planet eventually will fix itself, as it always has. That is the shocking but not surprising theory of a professor from Delft, called Salomon Kroonenberg, also called 'the climate-sceptic'. And of course he is right. Of the total history of this planet, human beings like us have spent very little time on it. Compared to the total lifespan of the planet we have been here for a very unimportant and negligible period of time. We will fade away eventually.... Or will we?

But that is not the discussion. We are trying to define what is needed for leadership to make drastic moves. When your house is on fire, you do not start a discussion about how the tasks will be divided to save as much as we can from the burning place, I hope. When the house is on fire we begin immediately to save ourselves and our loved ones and only then worry about our things.

No sense of urgency

So, it is very plain to say that the planet is not on fire yet. Of course, it is in the eyes of environmentalists, who probably are right. But definitely the house is not on fire in the eyes of the leaders. Because they do not move for some reason. There is no sense of urgency apparently.

And believe me, if there is no sense of urgency and no need to have a sense of urgency, there will be no action. That is the simple law of business.

That is pretty unfortunate because we need a sense of urgency. We need leaders to step up and set an example, or at least allow others within their company to do so. Because I can also assure you that in any company there are always people who want to make radical moves towards becoming totally sustainable. But having leadership behind you helps tremendously and leadership that doesn't care is eventually disastrous for any sustainable development within the company.

What did I say here? Radical moves? Let me give you an example of radical moves made by a man who started his company by making carpet tiles in 1973. A normal industrialist, coming from an environment in which he had been making serious steps on the corporate ladder. Just a leader like any other, of course with very entrepreneurial characteristics. But something strange happened to Ray Anderson after he had been successfully in business for over twenty years. By that time the sales of his company had grown to about 700 million US dollars. Quite an achievement, don't you think?

So, it is fair to say that Ray Anderson was a successful entrepreneur, even though he calls himself an industrialist. Why did he need to change anything? Well, he didn't, but he did. And there was no sense of urgency. He created his own sense of urgency. But why did he start to think about it and how did he define sustainability and how did he explain it to his people and how did he get them to believe him and follow his ideas? These issues are very interesting to look into a little bit more, because they are exactly the issues that all leaders face.

How did he come to it after all? Because his company, Interface, in 1994 was successful and 100% compliant with all rules and regulations. Nothing was wrong at all and they were very successful. No reasons to change. As he writes himself, Ray Anderson had to give a speech and in preparing for that speech about 'how sustainable they were', which was kind of an uncomfortable topic, he read a book, called 'The Ecology of Commerce', by Paul Hawken. And in that book, in a chapter called The Death of Birth, Ray Anderson read an indictment. Just like the one I described earlier in my speech to all of those CEOs. And suddenly he realized that while being an industrialist his company destroyed the very resources of this planet. It suddenly struck him, and I can well imagine, that something in his industry was seriously wrong. The message again and again in the book of Hawken – the industrial system is destroying the planet and only industry leaders are powerful enough to stop it – hit him so hard that he decided to immediately make a radical move in his business. He told his people that they had to be 100% sustainable within six years. When telling his people, he confused them terribly, because it was a different Ray Anderson speaking to them, with a totally different message. But he explicitly told them, we will keep doing exactly the same, making carpet tiles, but we are now striving to derive 100% of all raw materials and energy from renewable sources, be waste- and pollution-free, and have no environmental footprint in their global business. Wow, what a message that must have been. No wonder that many years later Time Magazine called him 'Hero of the Environment'.

He realized that when they started the program and the company had a turnover of about $700 million, 10% or $70 million was going down the drain as waste. And that's what they started with. They defined a strong program to bring the amount of waste down, called QUEST (Quality Utilizing Employees' Suggestions and Teamwork). What a great name. Remember Mars? Where they do not even have employees, but Associates. By the way, Associate means 'partner, companion, fellow' etc, which engenders a totally different feeling toward it than employee, particularly in the sense of FTE (full time equivalent) as is used in many, many companies.

Ray mentions some important things in his book, of which I only take two elements that I want to share here. One is that he, as a leader, started with a message in 1994 that was barely understood by his people. But he mentions the importance of repeating that message 'consistently and persistently'. Everybody must realize that the message is not going away anymore, ever. And in order to succeed as a leader to implement this radical view, one needs followers because it is impossible to do alone. Find followers and inspire them.

Leaders have to realize that sustainability does not simply mean whether something will last. As Michael Fullan defines it 'sustainability is the capacity of a system to engage in the complexities of continuous improvement consistent with the deep values of human purpose.' Understand that? Maybe we should try to make it easier to grasp by taking a look at how nature treats it. We then move swiftly into the area which Janine Benyus calls Biomimicry. A strange word which most people have never heard of, describing a new science that studies nature and tries to find out how nature's best ideas can be developed for human use and for business. Particularly interesting if we want to develop an environment in which, as Ray Anderson started with, no waste. Or as a Dutch waste management company Van Gansewinkel uses in their marketing slogan 'Waste no more', meaning that waste does not exist.

In nature there is no waste either, everything is part of a cycle, with no beginning and no end. That is something everybody should understand because we are part of nature. How then could we derive ideas to use for our business purpose? Without repeating Benyus I will give some ideas that strike me and that we are using in our own business in order to become sustainable.

Nature is a complex system that keeps itself alive if we do not interfere. The system, like any system maybe, will eventually balance out. All complex and mature ecosystems have, what Benyus calls, ten strategies to survive:

✔ use waste as a resource
✔ diversify and cooperate to fully use the habitat
✔ gather and use energy efficiently
✔ optimize rather than maximize
✔ use materials sparingly
✔ don't foul your nests
✔ don't draw down resources
✔ remain in balance with biosphere
✔ run on information
✔ shop locally

Now, how could these strategies help us in business? I am sure you easily recognize some, because some strategies are obvious, like "don't draw down resources". But 'shop locally' is even more interesting and intriguing. Take China and the booming business of outsourced production from Western countries. And why do we produce in China? Because it is cheaper, yes, very smart. Is it cheaper indeed, or are we fooling ourselves. Is it cheaper even when we take production cost, transportation cost, monitoring cost and all other cost into consideration? Yes it is, stupid, otherwise we wouldn't be doing it, would we.

But do we know how we are polluting China with all the factories there? Did you see the smog that fell over Beijing during the Olympics in 2008? Read about it and estimate how much the real production cost in China would be if we had to produce sustainably there. Yes, the cost would multiply and still we have not even yet calculated how much pollution is being caused by transporting raw materials from all over the world to the Chinese factories. And if we included the introduction of fair and reasonable workers' rights to the Dickensian working conditions in the costs, wouldn't producing in China become impractical and unaffordable? There is no need for financial experts to realize that as soon as all these costs, which are real costs, are taken into account, production-outsourcing to China would stop. This stresses the fact that shopping locally will eventually be normal. Production will come back to where the usage is, but that can only be done when materials are being used sparingly and waste is being used as a resource.

New leadership is daring and means several things. It means that new leaders, leaders for sustainability or sustainable leaders, have a daring task. It requires guts and it requires moving in different directions. It requires the ability to do things that are not asked for by law (yet) and it requires them to have a vision on the future.

Seth Godin writes an interesting and funny book on Dare! In which he states that for leaders it is not important to follow the status quo, but it is important that the status quo follows the leaders.

Suggested Websites
- www.vangansewinkel.nl
- www.vangansewinkel.com
- www.interfaceflor.com
- www.greenr.com
- biomimicry videos on youtube
- salomon kroonenberg on youtube
- www.salomonkroonenberg.nl
- www.biomimicry.net
- www.corpwatch.org
- www.corporateknights.ca
- www.desmogblog.com
- www.nudge.nl

Books
- **Confessions of a radical industrialist**,
  Ray Anderson, ISBN 978-1-847-94029-2
- **Biomimicry**, Janine Benyus, ISBN 978-0-06-053322-9
- **Poke the box!**, Seth Godin, ISBN 9781936719006
- **The Ecology of Commerce: A Declaration of Sustainability**,
  Paul Hawken, ISBN 0887307043

Steps to becoming a sustainable leader

1. Create a sense of urgency for your company; its leaders and its employees
2. Develop a huge poster in which you INDICT your own company
3. Put pictures of real people on the poster and spread it throughout your company
4. Organize discussion events about the INDICTMENT
5. Try to find a strategy to improve and neutralize the statements made on the poster
6. Find followers and start working on neutralizing the INDICTMENT
7. Evaluate the ten strategies of Benyus and see how they work for your company
8. DARE to implement some of these strategies; I suggest you start with one.

TAKING CARE!

RUUD SONDAG (CEO Van Gansewinkel)

INTERVIEW

'Sustainability determines the future of our company', were the first words of Ruud Sondag, CEO of Van Gansewinkel in the interview I did with him. Ruud, having been the CEO of this great waste management company for about 10 years, still feels the family DNA in the organization. The company by the way used to be family owned and that is how it got its name Van Gansewinkel.

The vision of the founder, Leo van Gansewinkel was that the business was not to collect waste, but to do something with that very same waste. That vision from the 60s resulted in the slogan the company is using today 'Waste no more'.

Interestingly enough, Ruud is using the same analogy as we are at Qurius, moving from 'back-door to front-door'. The vision that Van Gansewinkel has on waste and taking a broader role in its social responsibility has taken the company to completely new levels within their customers. Instead of talking to purchase managers about prices of collecting waste, the company is now talking to board level managers about cradle to cradle issues, circular economy and other topics. What a change the company has made.

Ruud stresses the fact that communication, repeating the story over and over again year after year, is necessary to convince the employees. But not only communicating, also translating the vision to each individual at his or her individual level is a necessity to get acceptance stickiness. 300 employees received a certificate after attending a training session about the Cradle to Cradle vision. In this way Van Gansewinkel ensures that employees have a role within the vision and the strategy.

Being asked how he personally still feels about sustainability, Ruud tells us that it remains his passion. He feels it to be great and very fulfilling to build a different company in its field. 'Everybody can buy waste trucks and build a waste management company, but it is good to see how both customer and employee satisfaction are going up by building a company that cares about the society it is an element of.'

Important is that the vision sticks with all employees and that it is not a personal hobby of the CEO. But because the sustainability vision creates real value, which is seen by all the people in the company, it sticks. The company has all kinds of programs to help its 7000 employees to get involved; using toolboxes, training and meetings about social issues are some examples of how the company wants to involve its employees. Taking good care of the trucks, cleaning them and making them the 'business cards' of the company is but a small example of the care that all employees take. 'Taking care', seems to be important words within Van Gansewinkel; taking care of each other, of society and of customers.

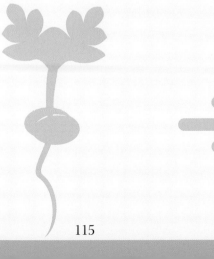

The sustainability vision of Van Gansewinkel seems to be supported by its large stakeholders, KKR and CVC, because they seem to believe in the long-term upsides of sustainability. It is not difficult to see how the company gets major commercial advantages from its vision. The broader role it plays in society shines on its customers as well. Companies and potential customers want to belong to the vision of Van Gansewinkel. That has helped the company greatly because there should be no misunderstanding that the company is very much profit-driven. But the margins are small in a highly competitive market of a commodity like waste.

Ruud sees a great future for the company, because the world of waste will fundamentally change in a way that fits the company vision very well.

Already movements like 'cradle to cradle' and 'circular economy' are beginning to show its effects on waste management. And since the price-rally on commodity prices keeps on going, industries have to rethink the long-term use of their commodities. Van Gansewinkel sees a huge opportunity in this trend.

One great example the company has is a group of customers who gave all their used and highly confidential paper documents to Van

Gansewinkel to destroy in a confidential and secure manner. In the past this huge load of paper was burned, later it was recycled to toilet paper (which only means a one-time recycling), but now this paper is being recycled to new office paper without using wood or any other toxic elements. The recycling of this paper is using 83% less water, 72% less energy, and most importantly this recycling process can be done 7 times before new wood is needed. Seven times this paper is used and re-used by the same customers. This is a strong example of circular economy, which gives Van Gansewinkel its huge edge over its competition.

In Ruud's opinion the linear economy of 'commodity – product – waste', doesn't have a future and Van Gansewinkel can play a huge role in this transformation because of its long experience with waste.

So true sustainability determines the future of the company!

Scan
me

"Human resources are like natural resources; they are often buried deep. You have to go looking for them, they're not just lying around on the surface. You have to create the circumstances where they show themselves." Sir Ken Robinson

TIME TO CHANGE

CHAPTER 9

'Our Time for Change', ' Stand for Change' and 'It's about Time. It's about Change', one can fill a book citing Barack Obama on change. Whereas he wanted to convince American voters, I would like to make an appeal to all entrepreneurs of all enterprises, small, big, doesn't matter: it's change we need. Not only because we're running out of natural resources and are damaging nature's balance. Not only because we're leaving next-generations empty-handed. Not only because the world needs improvement. Have a good look. Over the years you've been restructuring, cutting costs, working on efficiency improvements and by now you've reached the limits of reduction and control. You'll have to search for different ways to enter new markets; to connect to your customers; to attract good employees; to please your stakeholders. To use a last tagline of Obama – 'Change versus More of the Same', that's the crossroad you're on. And as you know, more of the same won't work. You need to find new ways to stay in business. In or out. Yes, it's in or out. To find these new ways, you need creativity in your company. And that's a problem, a real problem, because after everything you did to your people, the last thing they will do is show their creativity.

You see, finally this book is telling you the truth. You're stuck. Anything positive in this? Yes, you can change, right now, and if you do, things around you start changing too. All the people in your companies are creative and could come up with the most innovative ideas that can help your company. If only you allowed them. How? Break the usual patterns.

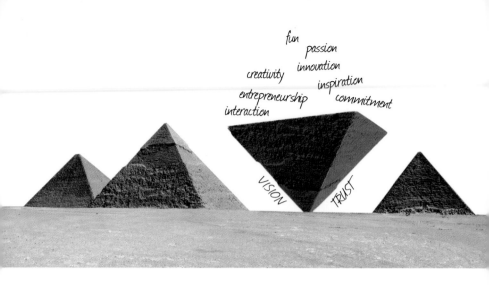

For starters, break with the parochial way we organize companies. Turn the corporate pyramid upside-down, that's what I told you in chapter 2. And I'll go into that a bit deeper. Traditionally in most companies everything is subject to a top-down hierarchy: the top decides what has to be carried out on the floor. And for years and years this has not caused any problems. Maybe we missed great opportunities, but we haven't noticed it because the markets were promising, results were good and people seemed to be happy. No need to tell you that these conditions have changed tremendously, which urged companies to cut costs and to work on restructuring and control. But did they change their organization models? Of course not, because they didn't even see this as an option. We've always worked top-down and therefore we never question it. Now companies are forced to break the cycle. They have to break with outdated organization structures to unleash the creativity needed for change. It's time for a new organizational paradigm, a new structure. An evolution from the pyramidal structure to an interactive living network. And whilst you're on it, breaking the hierarchy, start breaking the silos structures as well, in order to link all the specialisms within your company.

Don't get me wrong here. It's not the specialisms we have to break. On the contrary. Offering people the opportunity to work on the things they're passionate about is exactly what you should do. But have a look at how we've organized it – of course, in our over-structured companies we've carefully put walls between specialized units, in which there are specialists working, who know more and more about less and less. Not having a clue what their colleagues in other units are working on. Not because they want to. Just because we arranged it this way. Break those walls. Like at Eneco, the sustainable energy company. They broke walls, not only between the divisions and companies within the Eneco Group but also the virtual ones with customers and other external partners. They've even put it in their tagline – all for sustainable. And it's rewarding. If you do, people start working together, developing new ideas, inventing new products, business models and so on. Remember Eneco? They manage to build innovative and highly efficient windmill-farms in the sea. How? Together with others. The experts from many Eneco departments are working closely together with municipalities, science institutes, suppliers, the government, customers and so on. Only together is it possible to realize such innovations. Once you break the walls, you'll start making the transition to the creative economy. On the whole, our economy becomes more virtual, immaterial and conceptual. The generation of an idea is one of the most essential priceless resources in the new economy. Good ideas are worth incredible amounts of money. Ben & Jerry's started with an idea, The Body Shop started with an idea. Ideas – that's what it comes down to in the new creative economy.

Imagination gets you anywhere

Cooperation is key in the creative economy. Good ideas are never created by a single individual. There's always inspiration, interaction and exchange between people at the basis of an idea. As the idea of writing this book didn't come from my brains only. I spoke with so many people while working on turning my company into a sustainable company, and there it was. Not a coincidence, synchronicity. And with some imagination, a lot of cooperation and clear deadlines it became the book you're holding right now. In the age of creativity, imagination is far more important than knowledge. Albert Einstein made the distinction 'Knowledge gets you from A to B, imagination gets you anywhere.' It works the same for becoming a sustainable company. Imagining a sustainable company is where you start, and with creativity and technology you realize it. To give you an example – the new field of nanotechnology has an enormous potential. It allows for simple purification of polluted water in producing potable water, which is an essential resource for billions of people today. Imagination and technology, jointly making up the idea machinery, may save the world. The impossible does not exist. Okay, here I have to rephrase a

Becoming a sustainable company goes beyond imagination. Living Responsibility – as DHL puts it – is about putting sustainability into your company's daily practice. Check out www.dhl.com to find out how to make the transition from plans to action.

bit. More than 70% of change programs in organizations ultimately fail. They sadly do. More than 70%. Why? Because the changers forgot to change the culture as well. To become a real sustainable company you need to create a company culture based on shared values. A culture in which the mission and values are shared and standards and information inspire your people. A culture that offers the freedom to people to be your mission ambassador. A culture in which the P of Passion comes alive. Many leaders and companies pass on this. Not surprisingly, since changing the company's culture takes courage, guts and a whole lot of time. More time than the average time available to today's CEOs, as our entire society is still short term focused. Even when it concerns developing change programs.

Bringing me back to the first sentence – Our time for change. We need to change and make the time available for it. The company Mars managed to create the culture that enables their sustainable success, because they're realistic about the time one needs to embed change in the company's culture. Change takes a generation, but will not take place at all if you don't start. So start today. With yourself. Maybe you're the CEO of a company and you want to become a sustainable leader. Maybe you're not the CEO and you want to become a sustainable leader. Wherever you are in your company, a better culture starts with you. Put your imaginary goal in the timeline and go for it. And meanwhile stay open. Welcome apparently contradictory qualities. You need playfulness, questioning rules and laws, process orientation and room for experiment. And at the same time you'll need to be result-oriented, eager to perform and have a winner's mentality. Both sets of qualities are needed to become a sustainable company. They don't contradict. If you do it right, they go hand in hand. And don't reject all the issues that don't fit completely into your line of thinking, talk. Try to encourage brand new ideas whilst you keep in mind that the key issue is not (just) to generate new ideas, but perhaps primarily to abandon old and solid patterns.

   To conclude with a last piece of advice, don't be afraid to make one, two or many more errors. The most restrictive habit in thinking is to set new information against what one already knows. Don't. This is the perfect way to stay where you already are. Awaken people. Challenge them. Exploit nonmaterial natural resources like inspiration, pleasure, dreams and passion.

I know how it feels when you read all of this. It is scary. It is dangerous, because you might get out of control. But control is the most dangerous word in creating new environments A famous Formula 1 driver once said 'if you think you have control over your car when racing, you're not going fast enough.'

So I want to challenge you all; try for a change to reach that chaos point; try for a change to get out of control. I am sure that most of you will never get there. But then again... you never know!

Inspiring people,
there are many of them on the internet:

- Creativity researcher Mihaly Csikszentmihalyi
- Lou Gerstner Jr., former CEO IBM
- Tom Peters, www.tompeters.com
- www.ted.com

References:

- 'Competing for the future' by Cary Hamel and C.K. Prahalad
- 'Getting everything you can out of all you've got' by Jay Abraham
- 'Emotional Intelligence' by Daniel Goleman
- 'The living company' by Arie de Geus

PROGRESS BY PEOPLE

RONALD GOEDMAKERS
(CEO VEBEGO)

world
Improving
Entrepreneur

'We are curious!' is one of the statements made by Vebego, which is kind of funny, knowing that the initiative for this book lies with my company, Qurius.

Ronald Goedmakers is the third family member to lead this family-run company, which is recognized as one of the top-50 most sustainable companies in the Netherlands. It is active in facility services, health care and personnel services.

Like other companies I have interviewed for this book, Vebego is a company that sells a commodity, just like Eneco and Van Gansewinkel. They use their sustainable nature as a clear differentiator and Ronald really wants to tell the story. During the interview one can feel the passion and enthusiasm from Ronald for the story of Vebego.

Vebego started as a cleaning business in 1943, right in the middle of the second world war. In 2013, they will enjoy their 70th birthday.

It is the vision of the company that the world around them is becoming more and more transparent and companies have to be able to explain to their stakeholders everything they do. It is therefore important to treat your people and everything around you in a very sustainable way. This has always been a 'way of life' for Vebego. It is a matter of behaving properly and dealing carefully with your clients, people, and materials. The family, of course, talks in long-term plans and stewardship. As the head of the business and a family member, you do not own the company, but you have to prepare it for the next generation. This long-term thinking has become the culture of the company. Just 15 years ago, Vebego focused on clean products, clean materials and nature. Now that strategy has become more 'fashionable', but it is nothing new for the company. Ronald also sees the negative aspects of the widespread attention given to sustainability. In his perception it is unfortunately cheaper and more effective to hire an external consultant to write your annual report, exactly according to ISO or other standards, rather than to actually spend money on real sustainable projects and activities. However, because he is a very optimistic man, he sees plenty of positives, such as the social responsibility Vebego started to activate 7 years ago. The company created a Foundation in order to facilitate their employees to work on social projects like helping the very poor in Sri Lanka, Ghana and South Africa with their housing and sustainable living. About 300

employees out of the total of 46,000, have worked on these sponsored projects and have become ambassadors within their organization. As well as sponsoring these international projects, the Foundation supports sustainability within the company itself. And this Foundation is using 2% of the profits that are made by Vebego. One of the advantages of being a family owned business.

Ronald tells us that it's not only their own employees that are involved in the social projects, but also customers. This is a way to stimulate sustainability within the company on all levels, from manager to cleaner. One of the goals is to make the distance between management and employees smaller, so when Ronald participates in one of the projects abroad, he sleeps in the same room as his employees do. Walk to talk is his statement.

The 300 Vebego ambassadors, created by the projects of the Foundation, tell the story throughout the company, stimulating internal projects as well.

Thinking about the three P's, the most important one here is the P for People. The fourth P seems to be Ronald himself, with huge Passion for sustainability!

Vebego is a people company. They have nothing else but that. In The Netherlands they are seen as one of the top companies as far as sustainable employee programs is concerned. For example, they work with 3,000 employees with a so-called social indicator that means that they have great difficulties finding regular jobs. Vebego spends much of its time and research money in defining creative programs to define new services in cleaning. They developed an innovative program, which involves sustainable thinking in this highly commoditized and competitive market of cleaning (offices and other buildings). This results in a new service concept of day-time cleaning with cleaners online connected to customers and their own organization.

Bringing sustainability in dealing and behaving with people is core for the company. In a world that is changing, becoming more flexible and transparent, Vebego wants to make their cleaners more visible and respected. This culture spreads and helps them to keep good people with them and retain knowledge within the company.

Sustainability is used by the company to develop differentiating propositions to the market and they successfully achieve it. 'Bring people and responsibilities back to basics and be interested in your employees on a large scale.' These are the keys to the success of this second generation Vebego business.

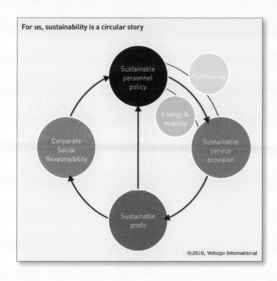

For us, sustainability is a circular story

Sustainable personnel policy

Purchasing

Energy & mobility

Corporate Social Responsibility

Sustainable service provision

Sustainable profit

©2010, Vebego International

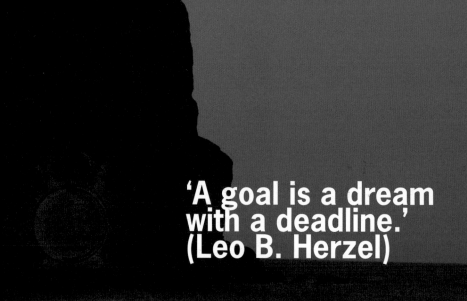

'A goal is a dream
with a deadline.'
(Leo B. Herzel)

GROWING SUSTAINABLE PROJECTS

→ Involve all employees or Associates
→ The planet will survive anyhow
→ The impossibility of turning a company into sustainability

It's like growing tomatoes or corn. Plant the seeds, water the young upspring and take good care of it. Protect it from the sun, take away the weeds and after some time you're ready to harvest. But patience is required. This short description would be sufficient for sustainable projects. Because building a sustainable company is impossible if one does not stimulate the employees or Associates to work on projects.

Within our company we very much stimulated projects to start 'in the field', as we call it. As I told in the first chapter – in our company we started being a sustainable company by letting the employees define ten projects they thought would be helpful. We start our projects with the employees to create a solid basis for stickiness. Sustainability has to stick at all levels of the company, not only the top level. Projects in which people are involved create the highest level of involvement one can get.

But the CSR manager of Qurius would be frank with you, 'there was of course some preparation and calculation done before we put the question on the table of our employees.' With a group of enthusiastic colleagues we started our sustainable search using ISO-26000. This is an international norm that describes exactly what an organization should do to be fully sustainable, or to be more specific, to be socially responsible. The good thing about such a norm is that you do not have to think anymore and can rely on the authority of ISO and the established commission in the background, which developed the ISO-26000 norm. ISO itself however does not qualify the 26000 as a norm, for the simple reason that it cannot be audited yet. I do not care very much about that handicap, because it is a very handy instrument to work with so you definitely should use it. So, with a group of colleagues we took a very good look at ISO-26000. We reasoned as follows; suppose that we would have an indefinite amount of money and time, which projects would we choose in order to get the level of 100% sustainability at our company? And we came up with many

'We launched Plan A in January 2007, setting out 100 commitments to achieve in 5 years. We've now extended Plan A to 180 commitments to achieve by 2015, with the ultimate goal of becoming the world's most sustainable major retailer. Through Plan A we are working with our customers and our suppliers to combat climate change, reduce waste, use sustainable raw materials, trade ethically, and help our customers to lead healthier lifestyles. Explore our Plan A commitments for 2010 – 2015.

We're doing this because it's what you want us to do. It's also the right thing to do. We're calling it Plan A because we believe it's now the only way to do business. There is no Plan B.'

At Qurius, we started with 10 commitments. Marks & Spencers started with 100 commitments in 2007 and extended its plan A to 180 commitments to achieve in 2015. Whether it's 10, 100 or 180, just start with any number of feasible commitments for your company and move on. Wondering which commitments to set? Have a look at marksandspencer.com/about.

projects to do so. Let's cover all the roofs of our offices with solar panels; let's use earth heat; let's start to hire mentally and physically handicapped people; let's forbid vacations to skiing resorts; let's change all our leased cars into electric cars; let's put only immigrant women in our Executive Board and many others. In this way, which was very inspiring I can tell you, we made our list of 25 projects that had to make us into the example of corporate social responsibility.

But this attempt was in vain, because it would cost so much money that the company probably would have gone bankrupt. We had to make a selection out of our 25 projects and we put ourselves under a strict regime meeting two criteria; payback time and self-fulfilment.

The first criterion has to do with the time it takes to earn back the investment in the project. And the second criterion has to do with the manner in which we can do the project completely by ourselves, without help from external consultants. Some projects didn't make it through this selection. These included the sustainable energy projects like solar panels, windmills and earth energy. Too bad, but these projects would require such a long payback time as well as the hiring of external advisors that it did not make sense to start them at that time. Investments of tens of thousands of euros and payback times of 10 to 25 years are just not good ideas for a publicly quoted company in the middle of an economic crisis. The projects that met the criteria were shared with our employees and we asked them to choose the projects they considered most helpful. Which projects would benefit our sustainable goals and on which projects would they be willing to work on in their free time? 10 projects were chosen. Ten beautiful projects that are making our company sustainable, have a short payback time and have the support of our employees. Although not every project got the full support of everyone as you will see. However, some projects enter right into people's comfort zones and touch their holy cows. So let's go to our sustainable top 10 projects.

❶ Carbon Footprint: the first project and the mother of all sustainability actions. Many methods exist to measure the CO_2 footprint and all these methods more or less do what you would expect from them. We have chosen the method used by The Climate Neutral

Group, because this methodology is fairly straightforward and easy to use. And besides that, mainly because we thought that the director of The Climate Neutral group is such an inspirational and nice guy. We made the footprints for every country in which we are based, including our Holding organization. To do that for the first time takes about two to three days per country and is quite labor intensive. When you make this measurement for the first time you bump into all kinds of small problems, like the lack of an electricity meter for a building, or a floor of a building. What you also see is that every country is inclined to have its own interpretation of the questions asked, which means that you cannot compare the numbers anymore. But when entering the second year, everybody knows what to do and it takes half a day per year per country from then on. When your first time measurement is ready you have the important task to communicate it to all employees and to define actions to bring it down. We defined about 20 plans to bring our carbon footprint down. In our company we have by far the largest carbon pollution with our cars. Fifty five percent of our total carbon production comes from our cars, followed by airplane trips, office lighting and heating. All actions to bring down CO_2 usage have to be aimed at these items. So let's move on to our mobility project.

❷ Sustainable mobility: employees in our ICT sector just love their cars to death. Do not touch these 'holy cows'. Do you know what you get yourself into when you try to make these cars less pollutant? We started by performing a 'hearing' among our employees to find out how much enthusiasm they had towards this topic. Well, clearly, there was no enthusiasm at all. People warned us that we should look for other items and we should not touch their cars. Our proposal to publish a monthly list with all employees, ranking the order of pollution, was highly advised against. It would stigmatize people and would be unfair. Nobody wanted such a 'top-250'. We would lose our position in the labor market, they all said. Well, we listened to them and decided to just move forward as we thought we should. We took some very clear decisions; all new lease cars should have a maximum carbon dioxide emission of 130 gram per kilometer. We also introduced the hated 'Top 250 emission list'. At the bottom of this list is one of our top managers, driving a highly polluting 12 cylinder car. He doesn't mind the joke here, and he can keep driving the car, because giving it back to the leasing company would cost us 25,000 euros. But this manager decided to compensate his emission by buying CO_2 emission rights. His new car will be an electric one.

The problems in our German office were even bigger. Our new (green) country manager inherited a huge 12 cylinder Audi A-8 from his predecessor. He felt extremely ashamed of this and hid this car far away. Also all other A-8's were banned from the company. Now we have a group of expensive and highly pollutant cars standing in our German company garage. They will be returned to the lease company against payment.

❸ Internal ICT systems: these internal systems have to be super clean, we think. Our computers have to be sustainable in the way they are produced, the way they use electricity and how they are eventually recycled. Our server rooms have to comply with the highest energy norms. We have to print double-sided, use the smartest energy lighting systems like LED, heating management etc. The nice thing about all these things is that they showed enormous results in the first two years, like the CO_2 results as well. We keep on going with all these steps, because you are never finished and when all employees get involved you can keep on winning.

❹ Sustainable propositions: of course all of our products and services eventually have to be sustainable. There are two sides to this goal. Firstly they have to be designed in such a way that they are sustainable when being used. That's also a necessity for ICT products. Software designers and programmers can make choices beforehand, ensuring that products use less energy and are less burdensome for the environment.

Secondly, we have to develop products that help our customers to become and stay more sustainable. Helping our customers to sustain their business through clever ICT solutions, that's the business we're moving in. Not easy though. Design and development of new ICT products take a lot of time and we have made many mistakes in the past. But step by step we're developing the propositions together with our customers that will help them to become sustainable companies.

❺ Diversity: Most ICT companies are, to be honest, racist and sexist strongholds. Doesn't sound good, does it? Probably they did not mean to be so, but they are. By the way, many people have no idea what the diversity of employees has to do with sustainability. And that is simple to explain. The traditional Western ICT hiring policy is aiming for thirty year old, highly trained males. But due to demographic developments this group of people has completely emptied out. We have to start aiming for totally different groups of people, like women and immigrants. In Dutch companies hardly any women or immigrants work in commercial or ICT positions. Of course there are exceptions. So, in order to be sustainable in the area of People and Profit, one should start hiring women and immigrants. In our company we discovered that we were racist and sexist in our hiring policies, without meaning to be of course.

❻ Customer dialogues: how often do you really meet customers? And with meeting we mean really talking about each other's business and ideals. Talking about vision, dreams, strategy, personal motivation and nightmares. Before doing business together it is important that people get to know each other and appreciate one another. In meetings with customers, customer dialogues we call them, two organizations learn to respect each other. These dialogues give us the opportunity to express our vision on sustainability. On this sharp intersection, innovative solutions are being developed and these innovative ideas can both be fun and lucrative for each organization. Just because commercial behavior is not allowed in these dialogues, they become the most commercial interaction one can imagine.

❼ Chain-dialogues: these meetings are almost the same as the above, but they are dialogues with your suppliers. These sessions started in the first year when we shared our vision of sustainability with our suppliers and discussed the ways they can participate and behave the same. The year after was a little bit stricter, since we were telling our suppliers that we do not want to do business with them if they are not sustainable. In the third we invite our suppliers to demonstrate their sustainable progress to us. If they cannot do it, we can no longer do business with them.

❽ Sustainable rewards: everybody understands the language that money speaks and we happily abuse that. The bonuses of our people will become dependent on sustainable goals. In a three year period we build up a 30% part of the bonus amounts being dependent of the goals set on sustainability. But also all other bonuses will become partially dependent on sustainable goals. In this way everybody has to understand that these goals are serious business.

❾ Sustainable reporting: I can be short with this topic. There are many formats in which sustainability can be reported, but GRI (Global Reporting Initiative) is the winning standard. That's why we have chosen to use this one. Most larger companies in the world are

Sustainability concerns more than your company's behavior. If you want to become a true sustainable company you'll have to sustain the chain as well. Go to ahold.com to find out how Ahold takes efforts to make sure that its suppliers meet the company's sustainability requirements.

using this standard to report on their sustainability goals. Mostly they do so in their annual financial reporting. But sometimes they produce a separate book. The advantage of GRI is that you create transparency for the outside world. GRI also helps you to define your vision in measurable goals, which helps a lot.

⑩ Health: the importance of health is bigger than anything else. In our company we want our employees to be both mentally and physically healthier than they were before they joined the company. We still have a long way to go. Step 1 was to take away the candy machines and change our cafeteria to meet more sustainable lifestyle choices. Many employees still are very upset about this step, because our CSR manager took away their candy and chips. Also, the veggie-burgers, which are sometimes served in our cafeteria irritate our 'Archies (like Archie Bunker in the famous tv-series)'. But do not let yourself be disappointed (or uncomfortable) by that, because we do not want our most important 'asset', our people, being poisoned by bad food. Over the coming two years we are going to offer annual medical check-ups to our people and sport activities during work.

These are the 10 projects we are working on. We started without exactly defined goals, but we all understood where we were going. Not only were the employees involved in this process, also our very critical financial controller was in it from the start, to ruthlessly check our rough calculations. Our also sceptical CSR manager liked the results of his work. He showed that our company can make hundreds of thousands of euros by acting on these projects and that we are currently making that money. One example?

In our first active year we were able to bring down our carbon dioxide over all of our 5 countries by 13.6%. Per person of course, otherwise the growth of the company would dilute the number. This reduction of 13.6% in carbon dioxide can easily be expressed in euros. They are liters of car fuel, kilowatts electricity, cubic meters of natural gas, airplane miles etcetera. We have used an external agent to calculate this reduction into euros and we found out that we saved at least 300,000 euros on this project alone. In our opinion this was astonishing! What a great result to make in only one simple project in the first year. Imagine what else we could do over the coming years and in all other projects.

But, in hindsight it is perfectly understandable that there is an immense amount of low hanging fruit in year one. Take for example the 12 huge lights that are illuminating our corporate headquarters every day. These lights turned on every afternoon at 1 pm (!) and nobody knew how to turn them off. These enormous lamps, 3000 watt each, illuminated our building for many years before and everybody thought that was normal. We just turned them off and off they will stay. Easy, yeah? Instant savings of 15000 euro per year. Easy money, don't you think?

Allright then – it is your turn to define your 10 sustainability projects and make money while becoming sustainable.

Interesting websites:
- www.globalreporting.org
- www.climateneutralgroup.com
- www.cdproject.net
- www.iso.org/iso/iso_catalogue
- www.carpages.co.uk/CO2
- www.car-emissions.com

google 'diversity in the workplace'

Books:
ISO-26000 The Business Guide,
Lars Moratis,
ISBN978-190-609-3402

The dynamics of managing diversity,
Anne Marie Green,
ISBN978-185-617-8129

Start with the projects that bring most cost savings

Take one year on a number of projects and use the evaluation to continue

CAREFULLY MEASURE THE **money** EFFECTS OF YOUR PROJECTS

Don't forget the CO_2 case in your first series of projects; it can save huge amounts of money

THE WAY TOWARDS FULL SUSTAINABILITY EASILY TAKES 4 YEARS OR MORE.

RELATE YOUR BONUSES TO REACHING SUSTAINABILITY GOALS

'The most
important things
are unknown or
unknowable.'
(Dr. William
Edwards
Deming)

TECHNOLOGY IS THE ANSWER, NOW WHAT'S THE QUESTION?

→ You can't improve what you don't measure
→ In God we trust; all others must bring data
→ Perception is key: look differently!

CHAPTER 12

The other day my eyes fell on an article with the heading 'choose your own sustainability index'. In short they'd put the finger on all those sustainable rankings showing different positions for the same companies. Where one ranking puts Unilever forward as the ultimate sustainable leader, the following tells us that they take the 52nd position in their sustainable top100. It makes one wonder and doubt. Not only about how sustainable the companies really are, but also how trustworthy all these rankings are. Before I go on to tell you the ways to measure sustainability, I want to take you back to chapter 6. Here I told you to start acting before thinking and not to get distracted by traditional planning processes. Set a goal that you haven't clearly defined, start acting and just move on and on and on. Once you've taken off on your sustainable journey, say after a year, you'll find time to evaluate the progress you've made and you can make more precise and realistic sustainable goals for your company. And there you go. Once you've got precise goals, measuring quickly follows. But how do we measure sustainable progress? How do we measure our environmental impact?

To measure the environmental impact of a business can be quite a challenge if it is to be accurate and stand up to scrutiny. There are simple methods, and they can be a good start, but unless you get a high degree of accuracy it is very difficult to get a baseline and therefore impossible to understand if your actions have generated an improvement. Let's consider just a few of the many many methods, none of them really right or wrong. For starters, the entry-level CO_2 calculators you find on-line. There are so many of these CO_2 tools on the web that it feels like a whole new industry is being developed, opportunistically, taking advantage of a current need rather than supporting the achievement of a goal. Some tools are better than others and if you wanted to just dip your toe in the water you might consider using the 30 minutes CO_2 calculator on climateneutralgroup. com. CNG is a social enterprise working with businesses to encourage small steps. The on-line tools are good as they generate interest and encourage you to set reduction targets. And if you repeat let's say every three months, you start to get a real insight into your progress. What this kind of tool does not do is consider all the other impacts a business can have; nothing for example on embodied energy or whole life impact, despite the simplistic field 'Other'.

Another site to consider is provided by the WWF. This one is aimed more at your personal footprint rather than business, but nonetheless it is interesting because it can be applied scientifically and can easily

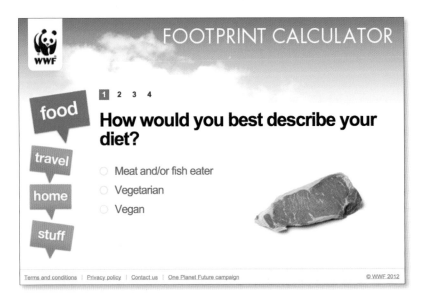

be used to change the way we think. The first topic it covers is diet. Why? Because, arguably, eating red meat has a greater impact on global warming than transport! In 2006 the UN stated that 18% of greenhouse gases are generated by the livestock sector. Read the book Time to eat the dog? by Robert and Brenda Vale, even if you are a pet lover! The other element of the WWF calculator that is missed by other tools is consumer goods. In the case of business this means mobile phones, laptops, servers etc. All that invisible embodied energy! 'Ecological Footprint'. Environmental experts consider this to be the most important and complete metric as it equates to the pressure humans bring on the planet. And conversely, the ability of the planet to support humans. It is a health-check for the planet that can then be applied to continents, countries, businesses and families. In 2010 the WWF's Living Planet report concluded that we need 1.5 earths to support the pressure humans put upon it. If we all lived the lifestyle of the citizens of the USA we would currently need 5 earths. Using the concept of Global Hectares (gha) the system takes the available productive land and marine area in the biosphere and, for each activity, calculates the number of those global hectares required to sustain it. So, the driving of a car can be measured in gha, as can the production of a beefburger. Take a look at footprintstandards.org for a more in-depth description and the well-defined standard.

To all of those who love a more mathematical approach, have a look at I=PAT. Paul Ehrlich (American biologist and author of the best-selling book The Population Bomb) developed this formula together with his wife, Anne, and other academics to represent the impact that the human population has on the environment.

(I) Human Impact = (P) Population x (A) Affluence x (T) Technology.

How to read this formula? The world's population (P) passed 7 billion in 2011 and is expected to reach 9 billion by the year 2100. Arguably, it is anticipated that it will stabilise as women are having fewer children and the earth can only produce so much food. The environmental impact of a growing population is increased land use, resulting in habitat loss for other species, increased resource use/demand and an increase in pollution. Let's move on to the 'A'. Over the last few centuries, the world's Gross Domestic Product (GDP) per capita has steadily grown. GDP growth is always seen as a good thing. Isn't it? Well, it can be directly related to per capita consumption, so no, it is not good. This is the 'A' for Affluence.

And finally the 'T', the Technology multiplier in the equation represents what we need to support the increase in 'P' and 'A'; the transportation we require, the labor saving devices in our lives; the expectations we have around heat, comfort, healthcare, security etc. Where does this formula bring us? We only have so much control of the multipliers. 'P' seems unstoppable, and who are we to stand in the way of once third-world countries enjoying a new found affluence? You only have to look at the populations of China and India, which together represents approximately 37% of the world's population, to see how they are becoming western-style consumer led societies. China has been building two power stations per week. Hello. Two power stations per week!

Ray Anderson understood the Ehrlich formula, but he had a different view and brought us his formula. If you are a military chief fighting a battle then you can lead your troops from the front, or you can stand on a nearby hill and take a different perspective. Ray did both, and his different perspective caused him to challenge the Ehrlich formula, $I = P \times A \times T$, which he rewrote as this:

$$I = \frac{P \times A}{T}$$

He put the T of technology below the line (a denominator), which has the dramatic effect of reducing the result. Why? Anderson considered the 'T' above the line outdated, so much part of the first industrial revolution, with characteristics like extract, take, abuse and waste. By taking the 'T' below the line, to be the denominator, he considered the characteristics would need to be renewable, cyclic, waste-free, benign. Taking this approach, Technology moves from being the problem to being the answer. So, how do you do this? For starters, by redefining productivity, which is primarily measured in terms of human productivity, or perhaps machine productivity. If instead you made resource productivity the main focus most businesses would see great financial savings as well as striking impacts on the environment.

Good manufacturing systems and analysing tools will help you in reducing waste and moving towards zero waste. Waste reduction is one of the most significant factors in achieving sustainability. The ultimate goal is to close the cycle by using waste as a source, as Van Gansewinkel underlines in its slogan 'Waste no more'. Where it obviously concerns raw materials, energy consumption and waste caused by travelling, you have to widen the scope and consider the whole-life-impact. A television program in The Netherlands about KPMG moving to a new sustainable building, whilst leaving the former building empty behind, opened the discussion about their true sustainable intentions. This underlines that on your journey to become a sustainable company, you'll have to put the standard higher after every result you've achieved. If you don't, your stakeholders will do it for you. Technology enables and helps you to take into account the environmental impact and whole life costs of all activities related to your business. The techniques are there to sustain the entire supply chain step by step. Being a sustainable company while your suppliers are not makes you an unsustainable company. Building a biomass installation to produce your own green energy is only sustainable if you trace the biomass you're using and make sure it doesn't cause a negative impact somewhere else.

Becoming a sustainable company offers the challenge and opportunity to question everything we do. And why shouldn't we do things differently, by being sustainable right from the start. Imagine a TV that, instead of having a relatively short life, was designed so that components could be replaced to upgrade it by the consumer themselves. Imagine a PC that could have its processer swapped for a faster one, or a hard disk replaced, without having to undo a screw and put your hands near wires and circuit boards. The companies of the future will ask these questions of themselves and design products accordingly.

My company is working on a technology that has been around for some time, but it is only recently that we have been able to make it commercially viable. Augmented Reality (AR) is appearing all around us, although perhaps not obviously. Satellite Navigation systems are probably the most pervasive example where AR is. It saves time, fuel etc. If you are running a team of field based maintenance engineers, covering high mileage, a good sat-nav system can create quite a saving. But imagine taking this a stage further. Imagine the parts delivery driver taking the spares to the site where they are to be installed, but then with the aid of Augmented Reality spectacles he is visually instructed how to fit the part – taking the place of the engineer. Imagine soldiers in a war-zone using AR spectacles to repair a vehicle, being visually instructed how to do it in real-time with no previous training?

We have this technology today and its use is limited only by our imagination. Spend some time and you'll soon find many more interesting formulas and ways to measure sustainability. But now let's have a look at the more precise goals I was talking about in the beginning of this chapter.

When you've been working for say a year on becoming a sustainable company you can start setting your sustainability key performance indicators. You define your goals exactly on the reduction of paper use, waste, mobility, CO_2 etc., whatever indicators are key. And I repeat KEY. You can measure everything and anything down to the smallest sublevel and if you don't watch out, the endless reporting, presentations and evaluations of all those indicators will kill the enthusiasm. That's also why I tell you to start defining the KPIs after one year of action. If you start too early with KPIs, the KPIs will kill the project because you do not know which ones will work for your company upfront. Your sustainable indicators have to be key to your organization, your industry, your strategy and your stakeholders. And keep it simple. Limit yourself to a small number of relevant, easily measurable KPIs and don't try to reinvent the wheel. When you're working on setting your sustainable KPIs don't hesitate to look at the sustainable companies in the rankings. The inspiration is all out there: The Akzo Nobel Sustainable Framework, the Five Priorities in the Ahold CR strategy or Adidas' Environmental Strategy 2015 and so on. Key, simple and easy. And never stop moving.

Actions

- Understand the scope of the carbon footprint you want to measure

- Decide if you are looking to just measure improvement against yourself or if you are aiming at a recognized target – is it going to be a robust measure that will stand up to scrutiny?

- Set ambitious but achievable short, medium and long-term targets

Websites
- www.footprintstandards.org
- www.climateneutralgroup.com

- Look for those one percent improvements

- And finally, if you're not a veggie, try it a couple of days a week

SUSTAINING PART II

ANDRÉ HERTOG
(Chairman Irado NV)

❤ world
🧍 **I**mproving
🧍 **E**ntrepreneur

For some companies sustainability is their core business. This is the case for Irado, a Dutch company specializing in waste collection and management of public space. Straight away, their business makes you think of the P of Planet, particularly in the light of sustainability, but talking with André Hertog, chairman of Irado NV takes us to the next level of sustainability.

Irado has made so much progress already on the Planet P. For Irado and its customers, mainly regional government offices and small businesses, the Planet P has started to become a commodity. Waste sorting, bio fuel cars, the introduction of a CSR performance ladder, and so on, they've already done it and it's all in place. The interview with André gives us insights of how to proceed once you've banked impressive sustainable results.

Irado will continue working on the Planet P to make further improvements through increased exploitation of IT possibilities. In the field of waste sorting for example, Irado is considering a digital system to monitor the content of its underground waste containers. This advanced and innovative system plans the optimal route and time to empty the containers. It means they make savings in time, money and CO2.

Another key improvement is sustaining the chain. All Irado's suppliers are screened to ensure Irado's sustainability standards are extended to include the partners in their supply chain. And there are dreams too: a bio-gas installation of a small heat power system generates green electricity from waste. According to André this stays a dream for now because it's financially not feasible and there's already a shortage of biomass in The Netherlands.

The real challenges for Irado however are on Profit, People and definitely Passion. In this book I've spoken a lot about passion of employees, but for Irado this is a key focus. Their 300 employees are working on sustainability every day and are well aware of their contribution. Where it concerns sustaining public space, Irado deals with questions like 'how to keep urban public space liveable and comfortable for the inhabitants'. Irado develops these sustainable solutions for public spaces and to make them successful they need to involve the inhabitants. In the field of the P of People, Irado plays an important role by offering job opportunities to people who are unemployed or are well removed from the labor market. Doing so, Irado increasingly becomes a sustaining company that helps people with reduced prospects within other companies, which brings a new dimension to their partnerships with local government authorities. 'To us, creating these labor opportunities is all part of becoming a sustainable company. It is in these areas that we define our sustainable goals as the next steps to the results we've already achieved on the Planet P.'

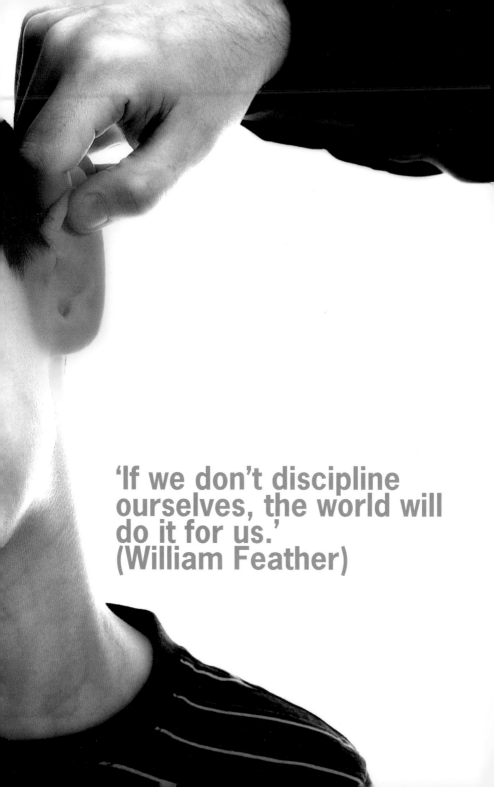

'If we don't discipline ourselves, the world will do it for us.'
(William Feather)

RELEVANCE; WHAT DOES IT MEAN TO YOU?

→ Speaking in your words
→ Translate and individualize the goals
→ Link the translation to personal perceptions

Simple things that are very close to you seem to be always overlooked. Simple solutions to problems are often not created. We are inclined to look for intelligent and sometimes difficult solutions. It is easier to find a complex solution to a problem than a simple one. It is a sign of genius to see charmingly short and simple algorithms in a software program, for example.

A couple of days ago it struck me. This simplicity. I had been stretching my mind over it for a long time, thinking about the involvement of people in sustainability. I have been mad, even enraged, when people did not seem to care about it. I have been so frustrated when only 10% of a company's population seemed to worry about sustainability. I have been thinking about mean ways to get the attention of other CEOs and to let them behave like me. What a childish behavior of mine that has been. Shame on me!

But I did not see the easy solution, which I learned from others, who mentioned it to me even though they may not even have been thinking about it. But the message struck me so hard that I haven't been able to sleep. Could it be that simple? Could it be so close to us that we have overlooked it?

The word is RELEVANCE. When it is not relevant for people, they do not see it; they do not understand it and they might not even care.

Could it be that simple? Translating messages in terms that are understandable for people is not enough. No, it has to have relevance.

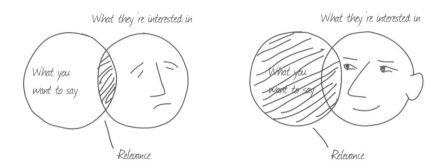

Relevance means: 'An item is relevant to a goal if and only if it can be an essential element of some plan capable of achieving the desired goal. This theory embraces both propositional reasoning and the problem-solving activities of people such as plumbers, and defines relevance in such a way that what is relevant is determined by the real world (because what plans will work is a matter of empirical fact) rather than the state of knowledge or belief of a particular problem solver (Gorayska and Lindsay).'

Wow, this seems like a difficult definition, but I can assure you that I did my very best to pick the most simple one out of the huge amount of literature that has been written about relevance. Probably without the purpose in mind that I am now using it for. But still, the above definition comes close to what I want to say in this chapter and the solutions that I want to give at the end.

We want to build sustainable companies; we want to build a sustainable world, we want to think long-term. But the 'we' in the sentence before is only a very small group of people. Sometimes it is a little disappointing to realize that only very few people, compared to the 7 billion citizens of the world, are worried about a sustainable world.

So, this very small group of people in the world, this less than 10% of the people of any company, want to bring sustainability into the company. And they mostly fail or face a hostile non-receptive environment. Why is that and should we worry about that at all?

Is it because there is no relevance? And yes, we should worry about that, because we seemingly are not able to relate to the worlds that most people live in. We are not able to translate our message, our thoughts, in such a way that people understand what we mean at all. And when they understand what we mean and it also has a meaning to them, they will move along. It's that simple, yes?

For example, a financial controller of a company understands perfectly that lowering carbon dioxide in cars lowers the cost of gasoline and thus can generate a tremendous saving to the company. The controller can be very enthusiastic about these savings, while not caring much for sustainability. Translating in his 'cost-terms' helps us in our long-term goals.

And a receptionist at the waste management company Van Gansewinkel understands the importance of being helpful and friendly to customers in order for them to come back and ensure a long-term future for the company. That's her sustainability, although she might not realize it. A technician at Eneco-energy understands the fun of new technologies and challenging solutions for new forms of energy, thus heavily contributing to his company's sustainability.

Translating the difficult and general word Sustainability for each individual is the solution to becoming sustainable. Otherwise we will fail with all of our enthusiastic efforts. People who read this book, people like you, are convinced and want to know how, or want to get the inspiration to go on or push a little bit harder. But people like us, we do not need to be convinced or involved, because we already are. It's all the others. I am sure that if we count all people on earth working seriously on sustainability today and set that amount off against the whole population of the planet, it would be a very disappointing equation. However, when we realize how many people are, each in their own way, working towards a better life and better behavior, like we all should, the number of people working on sustainability is substantially higher.

Let's go back to the topic of this book; how to create sustainable companies. Speaking about my company and the companies we all interviewed. Like I said in my introduction, the more we talk about sustainability, the more people get tired of it. And they should, because repeating the message over and over again, without thinking what it means to each individual, is bound to fail.

The overall goal is good and great and we measure the results and we even publish these in our annual reports. Good for us. But, as long as we do not make our goals relevant for every single individual in our companies, it will not stick and people will not go for it. And yes, that is the case with any goal. Remember the definition!

Linking the company goals

So, how should we use this knowledge? There is the element of translating our vision in terms that are understandable for each individual employee or associate. And then there is the fact that this translated message should have a meaning for the receiver of that message. It should not only have a meaning, but it preferably should also touch that specific person in his or her heart. Then we can ignite Passion!

For example, when we have set as our vision that we want to be 100% sustainable (whatever that means) we immediately have to realize that that specific goal doesn't mean anything to most people in the company. So, they just move on with their doings and don't bother. Disappointing for the enthusiastic leaders!

Pick up that vision and define per employee how that vision could be given shape in such a way that it is understandable. Quite often and maybe even almost always, the word sustainability doesn't apply here. As I said earlier, use cost-terms for financial people, use customer retention for service- and sales-people, use energy savings for truck-drivers, use diversity for human resources, use clean energy goals for research people, use customer happiness for helpdesk people and so on.

The goals that we are setting here should help us in reaching our overall sustainability goal, but per individual they are defined by their field of influence. This however still does not mean that they care! How often do people work with a set of goals that do not seem to bother them? That is, by the way, one of the main reasons that people do not like what they are doing; they do not like their jobs. That is because we have diligently defined goals for each individual, but have not linked these goals to their personal goals. Forget about any form of success in these cases.

As an aside, it seldom happens that every individual employee in an organization knows what is the expected output and when that output should be produced. Unfortunately so, because it would help any organization tremendously if every single employee knew what was expected from him or her. This form of output-oriented-management is basically what is meant by the new way of working (NWW) as it is preached all over the place nowadays.

New ways of working can be seen in many forms and shapes, but basically have not much to do with technology. New ways of working have to do with how people are steered towards a common goal, like in this case, a sustainability goal.

Most unfortunately, not many companies seem to understand the importance of linking the company goals to individuals, and even if they do see this, it is difficult to see how these individualized company goals associate or touch personal beliefs. I must admit that that is a difficult and time consuming thing to do, because it needs individual meetings with almost every employee. But hey, we have these meetings in our annual or semi-annual personnel reviews, don't we. Yes, we do, but mostly these meetings handle salaries and do not deal with tasks. This is a shame.

But, let's change that from now on. We will have to sit down with every single employee and present to him or her the individualized goals as they are derived from the overall company sustainability goal. We will have to talk and discuss with them about these goals and have to find out how we can make these goals relevant to them. What do they mean to them, what are their own goals in life, what makes them tick...? Yes, that's it, what makes them tick. What gives them 'shiny eyes', as famous conductor Ben Zander would say? And yes, then we are where we want to be. When we have seen shiny eyes in our employees, discussing their personal goals as they are supporting the overall company sustainability goal... Yes, then we have reached the ultimate form of commitment.

This might seem like a long lasting and intensive process and indeed it is. But as we have stated many times in this book, working on building a sustainability culture within our company is a very long lasting process. This element of relevance, as described in this chapter, is one of the most essential elements. I would dare to say that without taking care of the issue of relevance, you will never succeed. But now you know, so nothing can go wrong any more.

Websites
www.yesmagazine.org
www.odemagazine.com
www.newwow.net

Books;
- **The Art of Possibility**, Benjamin Zander, ISBN978-014-200-1103
- **Pump up your Presentation with Stories of Substance, Style and Relevance**, Jerry Weismann, ISBN978-013-276-3820
- **Making Sustainability Work**, Marc Epstein, ISBN978-157-675-4863
- **Strategy for Sustainability**, Adam Werbach, ISBN978-142-217-7709

Tips & Tricks

7 Communicate, communicate and communicate about this

6 Repeat this process every year or half-year to see how you are making progress

5 Watch their eyes as each individual describes his or her individual goals and try to link them to the derived corporate goals

4 Discuss these individual goals and try to give them meaning, relevance

2 Translate your sustainability goals in functional terms for each group

3 Plan individual meetings with each employee or associate and link these derived goals to them

1 Divide your company in functional teams, if that is not already the case

'SUSTAINABILITY MEANS EVERLASTING'

LUC VAN BUSSEL
(CEO The Alwaysbemobile Company – ABMC)

world
Improving
Entrepreneur

INTERVIEW

'Sustainability means everlasting' is the first statement made by Luc van Bussel, CEO of the unique independent automotive holding The Alwaysbemobile Company. This retail company is market leader in tires for all types of commercial and non-commercial cars in Benelux. Furthermore, the company offers full service maintenance, glass and body repair for its customers. Alwaysbemobile is working seriously on sustainability and its CEO speaks passionately about it.

The word itself, says Luc, defines 'long-lasting relationships'. Long-lasting with your team, your customers, your manufacturers, your environment, etc. It is a natural desire to be 'long-lasting'. A self fulfilling prophecy. A perpetual motion. Therefore, sustainability is very natural.

The big challenge for The Alwaysbemobile Company (ABMC) is to offer sustainable products and services to Benelux car owners that cannot fulfill their wants and needs without a car. Cars are people's best friend. There is no way to live without them. ABMC offers people an all-inclusive service offering to ensure they always stay mobile. It's in our name: The Alwaysbemobile Company.

In total 8 million Dutch car drivers are looking for a life without car troubles. Their main worry is the maintenance and breakdown. ABMC helps them to have a sustainable life with their cars. Well, I realize that for all of us this creates some kind of dilemma; driving cars and sustainability, what is that? ABMC is fully aware of the fact that this dilemma exists; but they have a serious advantage. The company exists

on the basis of franchising. Top entrepreneurs have combined to shape the company into the most successful automotive company in Benelux. These top entrepreneurs are highly passionate about their customers and their business. Good news for the customer!

Family companies in themselves and in their genes are striving for a long-term relationship between them and their markets. So, ABMC is also built based upon these strong corporate values of family based companies. It has sustainability in its genes... supporting cars and driving.

Isn't it great to have a company in this field being supported by family genes. How can that be beaten?

ABMC considers the P from Planet to be central in their minds. However, the P from People will never be forgotten. The people within ABMC are core and the most central asset. Just like at Mars, where, if you remember, they do not have employees, but they have Associates!

ABMC created a new Foundation, called 'Natural Mobility'. This Foundation is carrying out many projects that minimize the carbon dioxide, fill tires with nitrogen so it has far less resistance on the roads and doesn't make as much noise. This Foundation also supports what is called 'The New Way of Driving' and installs filters in cars to avoid soot. Do you know how many old cars we have in this world spitting out dirty soot into the clean air? How is this Foundation supported by the people from ABMC? Well, that is an easy one, because everything that is close to people and is important to them is supported by them. In this case the company does not have a problem motivating their people to support sustainability. They love it, because they understand. Ideas for new projects in the Foundation come from all over the place. From their individual franchisees right through to the headquarters, projects are instigated and inspired at all levels.

The company initiated a comprehensive book, called 'Infarct', describing how the country with the highest number of cars per square kilometer (being The Netherlands) could still solve its traffic jam problems. Due to its position in Europe, Holland is the gateway to and from Europe. Mobility is its middle name. This small country has to keep moving. But how do you handle the carbon dioxide of so many cars standing still every day (...in traffic jams).

ABMC is a combination of family owned businesses and that is a great asset, because all of these companies have a long-term vision. They all want to serve their customers with the best products for a very long period of time. These founders of AMBC want to be in existence 20 years or more from today. There is a long-term vision. And what does this mean commercially?

The company describes sustainability as a triangle; their sustainable, long-term future is ensured by permanent innovation... the best guarantee for the future is growth... and finally they only get their profits and yield through efficiency. And to complete the triangle, they get their efficiency through innovation. Sustainability, being supported by this vital triangle, is supported and boosted by Luc. And of course, the CFO of the company is guarding the efficiency. What a combination!

The family owned business operates mostly at local levels to serve customers on a super level. The headquarters of ABMC is working on a national level to ensure excellent supporting systems.

ABMC foresees that over the coming years the social element in sustainability will become increasingly important. After the P for People, which at this moment is essential for the company, the social responsibility will grow in importance over the coming years.

The role of the company in society will ensure its survival. For that reason the company is supporting the Ronald McDonald Foundation with 10% income from one of its major campaigns. Indeed, sustainability will be everlasting.

Learn more about Luc van Bussel on www.facebook.com/lucvanbussel or www.twitter.com/lucvanbussel.

'There are costs and risks to a program of action, but they are far less than the long-range risks and costs of comfortable inaction.' (John F. Kennedy)

NOW, LET'S GO

→ Creativity is difficult
→ Passion is the energy you need
→ Nothing can stop you now

After thirteen chapters you hopefully have been given enough ideas, inspiration, websites, books, interviews and energy to make a passionate start. Or, if you wish, continue your efforts with an ever stronger vigor.

Behave like a four-year old child now. Huh? It has been scientifically proven that people are at their most creative when they are four years of age. At that age you are not hindered by any hidden barriers in your head. The famous conductor Ben Zander said it like this: "You probably know these barriers as those voices that tell you that 'you are crazy', 'they are looking at you', 'this has failed before' and many other things. If you think, 'what voices does he mean here?', that's exactly the voice I am talking about.

I was giving a lecture some time ago and in the 150 strong audience was a group of grown up people with Down's Syndrome. At one point I asked a question to the audience, 'what or who inspires you? Any answer is ok.' Well, that should have been simple, particularly knowing that any answer is ok. But as you may have guessed, there were no answers from the audience, except for these 20 people with Down's Syndrome. They jumped up, started screaming enthusiastically about their inspirations like there was no tomorrow! After ten minutes I had to bring them to a full stop, which they happily accepted. Then I turned to the other 130 people in the audience and said 'and that, ladies and gentlemen, is how you are supposed to answer that question.' Don't start thinking long and hard, just throw the answers in! And that is what you are supposed to do after reading this book. Don't think, just throw all your energy in and run forwards.

Hopefully you felt my passion about sustainability through every line of this book, because I cannot think any other way. How can you ever run a company that's just there? A company that has no meaning other than to make money. How can you have a waste management company that's just collecting waste? How can you have an energy company, just producing energy, with nothing to differentiate it from all the other commodity companies? The word alone; commodity. Who wants that?

We are not living our lives just to live it and die. How dreadful it must be to belong to the 50% of people who have no clue why they work at all. I cannot blame them. I have to blame their management who don't seem to care and have no passion to give to them. Horrible managers, people without passion, what are they doing? What are they thinking?

I told you about the World-Improving Entrepreneurs; the people who just live and breathe sustainability; who do not know any different. It is not necessary to be such a person, it just helps to meet with them sometimes. It also helps to have them in your company of course, but not everybody can be that lucky. These are World-Improving Entrepreneurs, the WIE's as we call them at Social Venture Network, a network that consists of a very large percentage of these people. Wow, what a pleasure to meet with them!

Try to meet with them to get the passion. Go to places where they are, such as the conferences from SVN. Beware of the conferences, and there are many of them, where people speak nicely and formally about their great sustainable behavior, in speeches that are carefully prepared by PR people. Passion is nowhere to be seen nor felt there. And you know it, because you (don't) feel it.

Honestly, there are not many places to go to meet real WIEs. I will give you some suggestions at the end of this chapter. Invest time to visit them. It's worth it, I promise. Having World-Improving Entrepreneurs in your company helps a lot, because they are spot on from the beginning. It solves a huge bottleneck that you otherwise would have to face, ie. how to begin without support.

I told you how to build a team of people around you and to involve all of your employees or colleagues. Even to involve your customers. And to go one step further, not only involve your customers, let them determine how to move forward. But I would say that the most important message is that you should start without inhibitions, without any boundaries. Just go, go, go!

I did not give you any scientific examples of sustainability, nor did I give you any definitions (maybe except for the definition of Relevance, but even then it showed how difficult and useless definitions can be). No definitions please. And there are thousands of books written about examples of sustainable projects, believe me. So, also there I did not feel a need to bother you.

This book, if you boil it down to one point, is only telling you one thing. Is only helping you with one thing. The thing that is missing in many situations and therefore killing all trials to be sustainable. And that element is Passion. And that Passion is the Energy that you need to keep on moving.

So when I tell you to move before thinking, and when I tell you to go, go, go, how helpless can you feel when you read that! How helpless can you feel when you want it, but you don't know how; or feel lonely without any support; or feel misunderstood.

When there is no Passion, there is no sustainability in a sustainable manner. It starts and eventually dies. So, the title describes that the more Passion we have, the faster and the better our sustainable projects move forward. And did you notice the @ sign in the title. Yes, of course you understood that that is a link with technology. Technology that can play such a huge role in our sustainable projects. Remember Eneco, the company that came forward from a simple energy distributor, turning into an energy producer, but now moving into the role of energy divider between customers and producers. That company is evolving from a business with factories and all kinds of other hardware, into a clearinghouse based upon internet technologies. It is becoming an IT company eventually, being everywhere, anytime.

Technology is playing an increasing role in building sustainable companies. Wouldn't every company want to have a dashboard with which it can monitor its sustainability in real-time. And not only can they monitor it themselves at any time, but so can their customers and therefore the whole world. Talking about transparency, this is an important element in sustainability.

Considering that information technology is such an important factor it would be nice if the leaders of many companies would show some more interest and would not only see IT as a cost element.

What do you think about opinions being formed about your company? In chapter 8 we describe the new ways in which companies are being judged by their environment. This is totally different from  the past. Nowadays, people are connected by social media and their opinions are razor-sharp. Their opinions and blogs can be killing. I described in chapter 9 that CEOs would be judged in newspapers when they knowingly do NOT change the policies of their company. Remember 'j'accuse' from Emile Zola and the impact that had in 1898. There will be many 'j'accuses' in the future, just wait and see.

And sustainability itself, the word really doesn't matter as we have seen. The topic however is hugely important, but if people get tired of it, be pragmatic and simply use a different word. Relate it to the lives and passions of each individual and look at the result and work out how that result motivates and drives the people who create it. Link every goal and every result to an individual. That is what Eneco is doing in its business. That is what any company should do when performing its business.

But indeed, you are right, sustainability is a word that is used so often that it doesn't mean much anymore. Although that is a sad conclusion, we should not give up and we will continue to get results.

About the topic of offsetting, which should have been in chapter 12, but we decided to leave it out for the reason we could not agree on it. Offsetting, for example, is when you buy credits for the CO_2 that you produce. You buy CO_2 compensation when you bought an airline ticket, or you buy CO_2 credits when you drive a dirty car, producing more than 130 grams of CO_2 per kilometer. Is that wrong or right?

It is reasoned that offsetting CO_2 by buying credits is wrong and fake, but I am not so sure. Companies that are just starting sometimes have no way to quickly get to zero CO_2 production of course. In that case offsetting CO_2 production by buying compensation rights is better than nothing. Cars that cannot get out of a lease program should definitely buy compensation rights. But if buying off your whole CO_2 reduction program with compensation rights is your only solution to the problem you are a bloody coward. Pardon my English.

And wow, what a great thing the interviews showed. Everything, just like nature, is connected like a chain, without beginning or end. It really is becoming a circle economy. Also this book should be without beginning or end, everything is connected and it really doesn't matter much where you start. As long as you try to see the connection between the chapters.

The interviews taught me that most companies are connected when you look at them all closely. And when you connect them you see that waste is not necessary, as Janine Benyus writes in Biomimicry. There is a way in which all companies can be connected I am sure. Eventually that will happen, there is no doubt, because human beings want to survive and the sense of urgency will eventually come.

You should read the 'State of the World' every year, written by the Worldwatch Institute. This generally scientific institution with its dedicated president, Christopher Flavin, is one of the anchor points for information when you want to know the state of the world, as the yearly report suggests. In his opening statement in the 2011 report he closes with 'agriculture may once again become a center of human innovation, and the goals of ending hunger and creating a sustainable world will be a little closer than they are today.'

Although we barely touched on the state of the world in this book, I am sure that the state we are in is poor. I get sick when I think about the 'plastic soup', the huge part of the Atlantic Ocean polluted by garbage of which 80% comes from the land, basically our rubbish, which is thrown into the ocean. This piece of garbage is estimated in size to be almost 10% (!) of the total Atlantic Ocean. What are we doing?

But this book did not touch this discussion of making the planet green and the thousands of issues related to that. Many books have been written about that and I am sure there will be many more.

This book is trying to take a very pragmatic approach to making a start, by addressing a problem that is rarely addressed. Either we speak with sustainability enthusiasts who believe everybody thinks the same or we face skeptics, who do not seem to care. And neither of them is right, nor are they addressing the issue most organizations face.

And that brings us to the final piece; organize WOW and FLOW in your business.

We have defined the real problem as being the lack of passion for the problem. Its not the three P's that people do not understand, it is the undervaluation of the huge energy needed to pull through, or to even start with building a sustainable organization.

And Passion we get when we say WOW, when we are energized by great things. And FLOW is when we feel good, everything seems to be easy and autonomous. In every chapter we have tried to bring elements that help you to organize WOW and hopefully they are written in such a way it brings you into a FLOW.

When you have reached that feeling and you want to start moving with huge energy, this book has reached its purpose.

The book has to give you an unstoppable feeling that is so Passionate that nobody but you can determine your way forward. Go on:

Go create sustainable organizations!

Places to go to for energy

www.plasticsoupfoundation.org

Social Venture Network, www.svn.org

www.pinc.nl

www.worldwatch.org

www.ted.com

Acknowledgements

Giving speeches is my favorite way to spread the word about sustainability, innovation, creativity and entrepreneurship. Whether it's a speech for my company, Social Venture Network or any other business organization, it gives me the chance to meet many people who all have something in common – they share the urgency for change. Change to create sustainable companies as part of the sustainable economies we need.

And during all those meetings there are the recurring questions. 'Leen, I'm completely committed, but within my company...how shall I put it, they're not yet up to sustainability', 'I love what you say Leen, but how do we turn our company into a sustainable one?' and 'I completely agree, but tomorrow I'm back in the office and my managers don't believe in sustainability. How do I change that?'

These questions intrigued me. They made me realize that there are so many potential WIEs out there who are 100% motivated to start the change, but are still blocked by the 'how to' question.

To all those people who were courageous enough to pose these questions and share their doubts I want to say 'thank you'. It's those great people who inspired me to start writing this book in order to get you started. And I hope you've found the answers, clues, tips and tricks to get there. Start building your sustainable companies today, just like the associates of my company did in 2010.

In this book we shared a lot of the experiences and learning of Qurius' journey to sustainability and of many others. A collective journey that we've only been able to start thanks to the trust, commitment and contribution of all Qurius' associates – internal and external. A big thank you to all of you. Without the belief and support of our internal associates, previously called employees and our customers, suppliers, investors and other stakeholders we wouldn't be able to become the company we want to be – a sustainable company helping other companies to become sustainable too by smart ICT solutions.

'Collaboration is key', as I told you several times throughout this. And this book itself is a collaboration of many successful, inspirational and, most of all, busy business leaders. It is a huge undertaking and one that we all hope will inspire our readers. In bringing this book together, I wanted to call upon the specific skills and knowledge of some of the people in my team at Qurius. By doing this, I believe the book delivers a broader view of the messages that I have tried to communicate. Not only that, we have looked around the world to find and interview special individuals (WIEs) whose experiences of actually following their Passion has resulted in the successful, sustainable organizations they run. The People P in this book is no less important than any other and it is to the People P that have brought you this book that I would like to offer my thanks and good wishes. Without them and their fantastic vision, insight and actions, I would be dealing with a lot more theory and less on the actual experiences of other real-life WIEs. And that just wouldn't have worked for a book like this.

You need to see that what we are saying can really work, can really make a difference to your company, your planet and your life.

My thanks to:
Geerd Schlangen, my dear friend and Chief Brand Officer for Qurius, who wrote two chapters in this book about WIEs, the World-Improving Entrepreneurs we need so badly.
Jason Fazackerley, a great colleague of mine, who wrote three chapters in the book, giving it more depth about the planet element and required transparency.
Jeroen Verkuyl, my friend and our corporate CSR manager, who is struggling to perform sustainability projects in a company that is trying to become profitable as well. He wrote a nice chapter about his work.
Herman van Leeuwen, my very and always enthusiastic colleague, who wrote the chapter on the organizational change we need so badly with a great number of tips in it.

Besides the guys who helped me to write the book and gave me texts I could work with, I want to thank the people who I could interview, because they really opened up during these sessions and gave great inspirational insights. Many thanks to Marijke Mars, Luc van Bussel, Jeroen de Haas, Ruud Sondag, Giles Whiteley and André Hertog and

Ronald Goedmakers, from the companies Mars, AlwaysBeMobile, Eneco, Van Gansewinkel, SWR, Irado and Vebego. Great companies and as a result great interviews.

After writing a book the work really starts, some experienced writers say, and they are right. Alice Schulingkamp and Jack Gocher edited the text over and over again, in order to make it into one piece of work and also make the English wording right. Because, although I have lived in the United States for many years, my English needs many adjustments. But Alice did not stop with the editing alone, she got so enthusiastic about the book that she got involved in the design, the presentations and all other aspects of the book. Great work!

Finally the book then got into the hands of my long-time and very experienced friends of Barnyard, the design company. Marcel Boshuizen en Frans Mooren, sometimes supervised by Dirk Jasper, worked day and night to be able to deliver the book to the printer in time.

Final thanks to my publisher Eric Dobby from Global Professional Publishing, who again showed a tremendous flexibility in making it all happen.

Share your passion @ www.sustainablebusinessdialogues.com.

In this book you've read the cases of companies that have already made steps in becoming sustainable, such as Eneco and Mars. We have shared information about becoming sustainable from many different angles so you can start your journey.
But the story doesn't stop here. It actually starts here – with your stories. We want you to share your experiences, your ideas, what you have learned, where you have drawn your own inspiration, etc. These will be a great source of inspiration to others as well. So share the experience of your sustainable journey with other WIEs @ www.sustainablebusinessdialogues. com. Here you will find like-minded, passionate WIEs with whom you will make the sustainable difference!